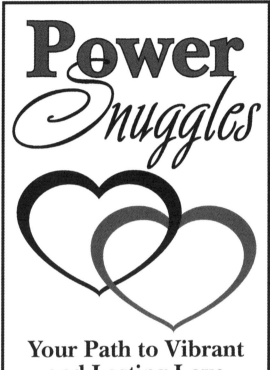

Your Path to Vibrant and Lasting Love

Jon and Beverly Meyerson

PELICAN PUBLISHING COMPANY
GRETNA 2015

The word "Pelican" and the depiction of a pelican are trademarks of Pelican Publishing Company, Inc., and are registered in the U.S. Patent and Trademark Office.

ISBN 9781455620449
E-book ISBN 9781455620456

Printed in the United States of America

Published by Pelican Publishing Company, Inc.
1000 Burmaster Street, Gretna, Louisiana 70053

Praise for *Power Snuggles*

"Everyone needs to read this book! *Power Snuggles* is a great guide to help clients improve their relationships, showing them how to move from Power Struggles to truly resolving issues. Their stories, examples, exercises, and advice help with the biggest issue we all share: how to communicate with someone we love, our opposite."

—Donna C. Fortney, LPC, advanced Imago Relationship Therapist; past president, Northern Virginia Licensed Professional Counselors

"I love the Meyersons' down-to-earth writing: entertaining, normalizing, and easily digested therapeutic truths ranging from neuroscience, Hollywood, and sports to everyday life stories. This is a book with the best of relationship wisdom that I can give to my family, in addition to clients, without appearing to 'therapize.'"

—M. Dorsey Cartwright, LPC, LMFT, CCMHC, past president, Austin Chapter of the Texas Association for Marriage and Family Therapy

"I find the book valuable in that it is co-authored by a husband-and-wife team representing Erich Fromm's differentiation between male and female perspectives."

—Rabbi Harold S. White, spiritual advisor, Interfaith Families Project of Greater Washington, D.C.

"This is a power-packed handbook of tools and techniques that can help each of us develop and maintain a loving relationship. Thanks for the gift; thanks for the toolbox."

—Dr. Bernard S. Arons, director of medical affairs, Saint Elizabeths Hospital, Washington, D.C.

"Jon and Beverly, husband-and-wife therapy team, exquisitely tackle most issues couples may experience with a story to which we can relate, accompanying humor, and a bit of analysis, and each solution to a particular issue takes only two pages. This book is a much-needed jewel."

—Rev. Stephen Parker, Episcopal priest

"I have enjoyed reading your 'Power Snuggles' newsletters, and I frequently send them to my couples clients, who enjoy them as well and find the guidance very helpful. Good stuff!"

—Margery Silverton, LCSW-C, director, Relationship Counseling Services

"This is an engaging book with nicely distilled theories that even the layman can understand."

—Judith Asner, MSW, BCD, LCSW-C, psychotherapist

"My husband and I have been married for sixty-nine years! It is amazing, even at our age, how often the advice in **Power Snuggles** gets to the root of some of our problems and helps us resolve them. We have advice for younger couples: It is never too late to improve your love relationship."

—Doris Miller, retired English teacher and wife

"Relationship lies at the heart and soul of who we are and what we do. In their book **Power Snuggles**, Beverly and Jon address relationship issues in a clear, meaningful manner, providing key insights into relationship stressors and practical steps to overcome that which threatens or undermines what we hold dear."

—Jane Ferguson, Safeguarding Coordinator/Support Person for Survivors, Spiritan Provincialate, Dublin, Ireland

In honor of our parents, who taught us how to love.

In memory of:
Sam Meyerson
Rhoda Meyerson
Roland Andelson

With deep admiration for:
Ruth Andelson

And to our children, whose love and support we have cherished through the years:

Tanya • Melanie • Noah • Julie

Contents

Preface

Over the years, we have guided hundreds of couples toward their goal of enjoying a mutually respectful, loving, long-term relationship. Couples, both straight and gay, come to us seeking ways to effectively communicate and avoid negative patterns they have witnessed in their parents' and friends' relationships. We work together as a team with each couple. This approach allows clients the unique experience of being counseled by both a man and a woman. It also provides us the advantage of merging our insights while supporting couples.

For the past five years, we have converted our ideas and beliefs into written guidance in the form of brief newsletters entitled "Power Snuggles." The newsletters were emailed to hundreds of our clients, colleagues, friends, and others who registered on our website. Our readers live in the United States, Canada, and beyond. The strong and positive responses we received from readers encouraged us to compile and expand our "Power Snuggles" into a manuscript for publication.

The book is structured around eighty-one Power Snuggles. Each Snuggle is organized into three sections: an introduction to the subject, often in the form of a dialogue, portraying a typical issue couples face; "The Road to Power Snuggling," which analyzes the issue, often including psychological research that pertains to the problem; and "Sustaining Your Snuggle," which offers guidance on ways to resolve the issue. Power Snuggles are grouped into sections by topic so readers can focus on issues that are most relevant to their relationship.

All characters in this book are fictional, with the exception of our own story in the Snuggle "Jon and Beverly's Argument." When referring to people, we use the pronouns "they," "them," and "their," rather than "him" or "her."

Our book is for those who are having problems in a love relationship as well as for those who have a strong relationship that they wish to maintain.

The concepts provided in *Power Snuggles* also offer timeless relationship advice for communicating with family members, coworkers, and friends.

Wishing you *Happily Ever After*,
Jon & Beverly

Acknowledgments

First and foremost, we wish to extend our heartfelt thank-you to all the couples we have had the honor of working with over the last twenty years. You have shown us how, through understanding and determination, your difficulties could be overcome, leading to much improved relationships and fulfilling lives.

We are also thankful to the readers of our newsletter, "Power Snuggles." Over the past five years your positive comments and suggestions spurred us on to pursue publishing this book.

Thank you to our agent, Janice Pieroni of Story Arts Management, for your unending enthusiasm and continued encouragement, which kept us going during the process of presenting our manuscript to publishers.

We wish to express special gratitude to our editor, Lindsey Reynolds, for lending your keen eye and providing invaluable suggestions and insight.

And lastly, a big thank-you for the support of the Pelican Publishing Company staff, including Antoinette de Alteriis, promotion director; Nina Kooij, editor in chief; and Paul Dean of the sales department.

Introduction

Rachel in Love

Rachel remembers that Sunday morning when Bradley's dog ran toward her in the park and jumped up, begging to be petted. Bradley scolded, "Down Plato, down!" and he apologized profusely, but it was too late. Plato had already drawn muddy streaks on her jeans.

Rachel had said, "No major damage. He's just a friendly dog." Then Rachel and Bradley began chatting. Their smiles and chitchat led to conversation at an outside café with coffee and sticky buns. Plato was nearby lapping up a bowl of water.

Rachel's thoughts return to the present, where she sits at her office desk. She pictures Bradley's smile and how he holds her hand and speaks so engagingly about so many subjects. They have been dating for eight weeks. Actually, it has been seven weeks and five days, but Rachel likes the idea of eight weeks since that means almost two months. Now it's Friday so they have ahead of them another full weekend together.

Rachel cannot imagine they will ever part, but her best friend, Kathy, had once been this in love. Now Kathy and her husband, Dan, argue right in front of her. Rachel and Bradley might marry and live together for the rest of their lives. However, to stay happily married, they will need to minimize their "Power Struggles" of couples like Kathy and Dan and learn to "Power Snuggle."

Power Struggles

A Power Struggle is a disagreement that evolves into an argument. Each partner tries to "win" the argument, believing they are right. Each tries to control the other. Rather than listening, they up the ante to prove their point. They may become angry, tense, and loud. They feel stress throughout their bodies, causing both mental and physical damage.

During Power Struggles there is no winner. Even the apparent winner loses since their partner becomes resentful and tries to get even, compounding the turmoil. Because partners are not working toward a resolution by listening to each other, these conflicts may continue for months or years. If conflicts occur frequently, they may lead couples to the point where their relationship cannot be salvaged.

The following narrative illustrates a relatively simply Power Struggle:

> BILL: Oh no! I forgot to use the 20 percent off coupon at the store.
> JILL: I can't believe you forgot to use it. You always forget things like that. You know we're tight on money!
> BILL: Why didn't you remind me? And I don't always do it. You know, you're not perfect. Last week, you lost the key to the file cabinet, and it took us a day to find it.

Power Snuggles

A joyful, long-term relationship requires that we minimize Power Struggles and increase Power Snuggles. Power Snuggling practices loving behaviors, building safety and trust, which will temper difficult situations. Disagreements are unavoidable; however, by listening intently to each other and being open to each other's suggestions, our collective ideas will lead to agreeable decisions. Power Snuggles focus on the "we" instead of the "me."

Through Power Snuggles, love and affection will abound as we merge our best ideas and accept each other's imperfections, understanding that no one is perfect. Power Snuggling allows us to grow by learning from each other, becoming best friends as well as lovers.

The following illustrates a relatively simple Power Snuggle:

> BILL: Oh no! I forgot to use the 20 percent off coupon at the store.
> JILL: No problem. I know you have a lot on your mind. I'll use it on Thursday when I go out.
> BILL: Thanks, Hon. *(They hug.)*

We have worked with hundreds of couples who were looking for ways to connect without daily conflicts. Through Power Snuggling, we have shown them how to capture the joy of long-term love, an even deeper form of love than the romantic love that initially attracts couples. The ideas and communication skills described in this book have worked successfully for most couples, as well as for singles seeking a loving relationship. If you are willing to try some new ideas, you too can realize the deep, loving couplehood you and your partner deserve.

I

When Love Feels Safe and Warm

When love feels safe, our minds and our bodies are free to expand. Whatever we say and do in our relationship feels right. We are connected to our partner and our partner to us. We have a strong desire to please each other.

Feeling Safe

It's a rainy Saturday and Teri is visiting Kenny. The best friends are in second grade. They make a tent by draping a blanket over a table. Crawling into their hideout, the two whisper as they sip hot chocolate and crunch oatmeal cookies.

TERI: Now we're invisible. Grownups can't see us.

KENNY: But we can peek out and see them and hear the funny things they say.

TERI: We can do whatever we want, and no one can say no. We can fly to Paris and talk French.

KENNY: And if anyone tries to stop us, I'm gonna push them down and save you.

TERI: Once we get to Paris, we can ride up the big tower.

KENNY: And we'll eat real French foods like French toast.

TERI: Yeah, and French fries!

The Road to Power Snuggling

Children are drawn to those things that make them feel safe. When parents argue, kids run into a closet. They gravitate toward a parent or a grandparent who accepts them. They distance themselves from those who are critical. Even as adults, we seek that same sense of safety. We all strive to balance our adult independence with that innate need to feel safe that drove us as children. Unfortunately, our relationships do not always provide the security we desire. When we are with our partner, we may feel we need to walk on eggshells and worry that we will be criticized for saying or doing the wrong thing. The relationship feels uncomfortable, causing anxiety and physical ailments, in stark contrast to the wellbeing and happiness we derived from our partner when our relationship was new.

Early in our relationship, we feel comfortable, and our words come easily. We express ourselves openly, feeling safe. In this new beginning, we are eager to please each other, scheduling enjoyable activities together. We fully accept our partner, overlooking small annoyances. This acceptance energizes us, igniting our senses. Feeling loved and safe, we readily display kindness and affection, hoping our relationship will last forever.

After we establish a long-term relationship, we must deal with daily life activities such as balancing checkbooks and diapering babies. This causes tension, leading to conflicts. We become less accepting of each other. We begin to worry that what we say or do will anger or alienate our partner. We stop sharing our thoughts and feelings, and our relationship suffers.

We need to return to the openness and acceptance of when we first fell in love. When we begin to share our innermost thoughts, accepting our vulnerability, and when we find ways to accept our partner's quirks, our love grows deeper. We can then again enjoy the safety we experienced when we first met.

The actor Paul Newman died in 2008. He was married to actress Joanne Woodward for more than fifty years. A few months after their golden wedding anniversary, they still felt safe in their relationship. Paul revealed in a *Hello!* magazine interview celebrating the milestone, "Joanne has always given me unconditional support in all my choices and endeavors, and that includes my race car driving which she deplores. To me, that's love" ("Paul Newman and Wife Joanne Celebrate 50 Years of Marriage," January 29, 2008). His wife famously remarked, "Sexiness wears thin after a while, and beauty fades but to be married to a man who makes you laugh every day, ah, now that's a real treat."

As Paul Newman and Joanne Woodward demonstrate, being safe in a love relationship means being ourselves, knowing that our thoughts and actions will be accepted. It means saying how we feel since we know our partner will understand. It means we can speak to our partner in a way that will not offend, even if we are upset. It means that if we make a mistake, we can admit it, knowing our partner will understand and still love us. We will be consoled instead of blamed. Being safe means we can reach for a hug, and it will be there.

Sustaining Your Snuggle

Remember when you and your partner first met and how you came to trust each other? What was it about your new relationship that prompted you both to be open and share your lives? If you no longer experience that feeling of safety, what is missing now?

Think how wonderful it would be to recapture those warm, fuzzy feelings. Begin your path back to togetherness by being more accepting of each other's ways. Develop a plan to create a "safety nest," a household where you support each other. In your safety nest, you should feel confident that when there are differences, you will listen to each other and resolve problems. Overlook some of the imperfections you notice in your partner. Start reconnecting by showing curiosity in their interests. Validate their ideas, and you will cultivate trust. Initiate changes in your behavior, even if your partner is not yet on board. They will follow when they start to feel safe again and trust you.

How We Learn to Love

It's Sunday morning. Andrea and Aaron's children are visiting friends. The couple is enjoying rare, quiet moments as they cuddle, sharing personal thoughts and ignoring the dishes in the sink and the overgrown lawn.

ANDREA: It's so cozy being held by you, Aaron. This is one of my favorite times. I feel as safe as a baby.
AARON: Well, this is the safest place for me too, Honey. I can't think of anywhere else I'd rather be right now. I could stay like this forever.

The Road to Power Snuggling

As infants, we felt the safety of our caretakers' arms. With few words spoken, we searched our mother's or father's eyes, felt their touch, and connected as a loving "we" rather than a solitary "me." Dr. Daniel Siegel, clinical professor of psychiatry at UCLA, explains that these early intimate emotions are indelibly stored in our brain. We relate to them as we search for future intimate connections.

Though romantic love is quite different than the love between a child and parent, we all yearn to recapture that feeling of safety and unconditional love that we enjoyed as an infant. When we bond with a partner, these intimate feelings reoccur. At all ages of our life, we strive to regain this connection. We even call our soulmate "Baby" or "Babe" to accentuate our love.

We desire this feeling of safety and familiarity so much that when we are rejected, it is extremely painful. In fact, brain imaging conducted by Naomi Eisenberger, associate professor of psychology at UCLA, indicates that when we are rejected, we feel a pain in the same area of the brain as we do when we are physically injured, often with greater intensity.

Research also shows that "the brain is constantly rewiring itself" based on our daily personal interactions, providing us with information that helps us to decide whether it is wise to seek or avoid bonding with a particular love partner (Diane Ackerman, "The Brain on Love," *New York Times,* March 24, 2012). When we meet our true love, our feelings of safety and initial comfort with the world reestablish itself. Additional neurons grow, and our love becomes even more powerful. Knowing that our brain is not limited to the neurons with which we were born, it is never too late to reestablish our love with our partner if that initial love begins to ebb. This provides us with new opportunities within our relationship to reignite the spark of love.

Sustaining Your Snuggle

How can you stimulate a romance that has become isolated and dull? When you first met your partner, you exchanged new ideas. You introduced each other to rituals and even persuaded the other to try different foods and environments. Love grew quickly and easily with these fresh, invigorating experiences. Your bonding felt complete. The challenge for your long-term relationship is to find ways to breathe new life into it.

Think of your partnership as a new beginning. Give it the attention it deserves. Begin by thinking as "we" instead of "me." Look for exciting experiences to share. Snuggling requires that you provide each other with daily positive support so that your brain can be rewired to again feel safe and accepted.

The Beauty of Two

In January 2013, Americans Bob and Mike Bryan became the most successful men's pair in Grand Slam history when they won their thirteenth doubles tennis title at the Australian Open. These professional tennis players are identical twin brothers. Neither Bob nor Mike has the best serve, the best forehand, or the best backhand in tennis. They don't even come close to the top players. However, they have done something that no world champion—including Rod Laver, Pete Sampras, Andre Agassi, Novak Djokovic, Roger Federer, or Rafael Nadal—has ever done. Together, the Bryan brothers hold the world record for the number of professional doubles tennis tournament titles ever won: more than 100! And they haven't yet retired.

When they were younger, Bob and Mike stopped playing singles tournaments because they found competing with each other for higher rankings was wreaking havoc on their relationship. To say they are best friends is an understatement, and merging their talents brought success. Bob, the lefty, has a more powerful serve and forehand; Mike, the righty, takes more balls on the rise and has a better return of serve. Their extraordinary teamwork allows them to intuitively know which brother has the most effective shot for each situation. They also know where the other will be moving, so opponents cannot find them out of position. The *New York Times* confirms, "What's remarkable about the Bryans' play is the way it integrates not only their strengths but also their weaknesses, mostly through their unique relationship" (Eric Konigberg, "Unseparated since Birth," August 24, 2009).

The Road to Power Snuggling

Applying the Bryan twins' model as a guide for our own relationship, we can use strengths and weaknesses to our advantage. When our partner does not measure up in any given area, we can quietly acknowledge their struggle, gracefully picking up the tempo by helping out or taking over if necessary. They will appreciate our easygoing approach to lending a hand.

Relationships flourish when partners are quick to praise the other's behavior. We chose our partner because we were attracted to certain characteristics. We must continue recognizing the strengths and talents that first attracted us to them and share their enthusiasm when they succeed.

Sustaining Your Snuggle

Think about times your relationship was working smoothly. It might have been yesterday or months ago. Recall those times when you shared laughter, supported one another in raising your children, or worked together planning a trip. How did you connect and support each other during those seamless stretches?

Now think of times when either of you were having difficulties and could have used help from the other. How did you each respond? Were you there for your partner, offering positive reinforcement?

When differences arise, consider what you can do to alleviate the tension, perhaps just by listening and validating each other. Aim for integrating your strengths and weaknesses while at the same time minimizing competition. Take time to tell your partner what you admire about them. Accept their faults. If these shortcomings cause difficulty, phrase your comments as "I" messages and explain how you are feeling without devaluing your partner. For example, share with your partner how you feel about them being late by stating, "I was upset when I had to wait in the cold, and we had agreed to leave at six." Using "I" in your message communicates facts or feelings in a way that is nonthreatening, whereas starting a message with "you" tends to imply blame, putting your partner on the defensive.

With these steps, you can work toward achieving the beauty of two.

The Simplest Way to Warm a Relationship

Kara could see right away that Dustin had had an awful day. He walked in with his usual paint-splattered overalls and held his lips tight. He looked down at the floor, shaking his head. "You wouldn't believe the number of times she changed the paint color. First she tells us it looks perfect, so the crew gets ready to leave. But then she runs out and says, 'It's a bit too pale. We need another coat with a touch of yellow to brighten it up.' And after that she says, 'If you could just paint it a bit darker, that might work.'"

Kara realizes that Dustin needs more than listening. She hugs him, ignoring the smell of the paint. He hugs her back, his body and face relaxing. He looks at her with a soft smile and says, "I love your hair. It sure is shiny today."

The Road to Power Snuggling

For months after we are born, most of the love we receive is through touch. Touch is our first language and our first sense. This most basic of intimacies almost always succeeds in comforting or reassuring the one you love. A warm touch releases oxytocin, a hormone that creates a sensation of trust. Whether we are days old or decades, touch improves our mood and makes us feel loved.

Studies have shown that touch can reduce blood pressure and heart rate, diminish depression, ease pain, and reduce anxiety. One study showed that a sympathetic touch from a doctor left people with the impression that their doctor's visit had lasted twice as long as it actually did.

In 2009, at DePauw University, Matthew Hertenstein demonstrated that we have an innate ability to decode emotions via touch alone. He had volunteers touch a blindfolded stranger. Through only their sense of touch, they were able to communicate eight different emotions, including gratitude, disgust, and love, with 70 percent accuracy. "We found that there are many different ways to indicate a given emotion through touch," Hertenstein notes (Benedict Carey, "Evidence That Little Touches Do Mean so Much," *New York Times,* February 22, 2010).

Sustaining Your Snuggle

During your infancy and youth, you were held tenderly. Think of the first time you were held romantically. Now remember the first time you and your partner held each other. Each memory stirs you with feelings of warmth and safety.

Today you can use touch to bring your partner closer. When words fail and your partner's facial expressions are unclear, a gentle, loving touch will speak a thousand words. It does not need to be a hug or a kiss. A mere touch on the shoulder permeates one's nervous system. It is simple and it works.

Visualize the benefits of empathic touch. Then at various times, take the opportunity to touch your partner in different ways, allowing warm feelings to flow between you.

The Magic Potion of Music

You may say I'm a dreamer
But I'm not the only one
I hope someday you'll join us
And the world will be as one . . .
("Imagine," written and sung by John Lennon)

I dreamed that love would never die
I dreamed that God would be forgiving
Then I was young and unafraid
And dreams were made and used and wasted
There was no ransom to be paid . . .
("I Dreamed a Dream," from *Les Miserables)*

Turn around
Every now and then
I get a little bit lonely
And you're never coming round . . .
("Total Eclipse of the Heart," sung by Bonnie Tyler)

Wise men say only fools rush in
But I can't help falling in love with you
Shall I stay
Would it be a sin
If I can't help falling in love with you . . .
("I Can't Help Falling in Love with You," sung by Elvis Presley)

* * *

Sandra and Jimmy sit in a restaurant after a difficult week at work and some bickering at home. They finally hired a babysitter so they could unwind.

SANDRA: Not too many restaurants call themselves diners anymore.
JIMMY: And not many have small jukeboxes like these at the tables. Hey, they have our song! (*He slides two quarters into the box and they listen.*)

SANDRA: I'd love to download some of these old songs for us.
JIMMY: Yeah, that would be cool.

Sandra and Jimmy listen as the music brings back memories. The week's problems seem to dissolve. He reaches over and takes her hand. She smiles dreamily as she remembers their first date.

The Road to Power Snuggling

Music is a universal language that transcends all peoples, cultures, eras, and sentiments. It is one of the easiest ways for us to relate to our partner and express a range of emotions. We don't always have the same musical taste as our partner, but more often than not, we find songs to share that we both enjoy.

Music feeds into the amygdala of the brain, which processes memories and emotional reactions. Simply hearing a few words or tones of a familiar song enables brain neurons to trigger warmth throughout our body's nervous system. When two people hear the same favorite song together, their memories are played back and love connections are strengthened.

Sustaining Your Snuggle

When did you last relax together with music that you both enjoy? What feelings did that experience evoke? Allow time after a hectic day to unwind together and listen to music that suits your mood.

Background music can provide a calm ambience that enhances your dinner, even when children are present to lend their rambunctious energy. Make time to enjoy your favorite tunes at home, at clubs, or at concerts. Get those brain neurons to stimulate warmth and positive feelings.

Dancing is a great way to combine the positive effects of music with the sense of touch that enhances emotional closeness. And it need not be reserved for dance floors and nights out. Kick up your heels at home in the living room or family room when the spirit beckons or dance around the kitchen while preparing dinner. Experience the upbeat results.

What Are Your Daily Highs and Lows?

Just before dinner Holly, Travis and Lori's neighbor, stops by to drop off mail that was mistakenly delivered to her. Holly hands Lori the mail and glances at their dinner table.

HOLLY: Wow! You light candles for dinner?
LORI: Uh-huh. Every night.
HOLLY: That's beautiful! We just light ours on special occasions.

Holly leaves, and Travis and Lori smile. Every night for the six years they have been married, the two relax in their family room before dinner, even for just a few minutes, to share their highs and lows of the day. Except for weekends, this lull before dinner is often the only time they have to share their day or plan for future events. They take turns conversing about work or any issues that pop up, both good and bad. This quiet ritual allows them to keep in touch with each other's activities, thoughts, and feelings. After regrouping, they go into the dining room to light candles and have dinner.

The Road to Power Snuggling

Though most relationships include celebrating major holidays, establishing our unique rituals provides us with a special feeling of continuity and security. In his research, Ernest Burgess, sociology professor at the University of Chicago, found that individual traditions acquire an aura of spirituality that develops intuitively and is critical in maintaining long-term relationships. Dr. John Gottman reiterates this idea in his book, *The Seven Principles for Making Marriage Work*. He writes about his seventh principle, the Creation of Shared Meaning: "Marriage isn't just about raising kids, splitting chores, and making love. It can also have a spiritual dimension that has to do with creating an inner life together—a culture rich with symbols and rituals" ([New York: Three Rivers Press, 1999], 243-58).

With so much uncertainty and fear in the world and our own hectic daily schedules, it is crucial to plan a regular bonding time. Except for special circumstances, we should expect to dine with our partner every night, minus the TV, cell phones, and emails. Power Snuggling requires that we consciously establish traditions that support our love relationship.

Sustaining Your Snuggle

There are countless rituals that couples can establish to help them feel that their family is special. Implement special traditions, such as the following, to keep your relationship strong:

- Reserve an evening each week as "date night";
- Prepare a special breakfast on Sunday mornings;
- Say something loving to your partner whenever they leave for work;
- Take walks together, stopping by a favorite coffee shop;
- View family photos and reminisce;
- Prepare food together in different ways; or
- Each week, leave a note with a loving message.

Not only do the rituals benefit your relationship, but children also love anticipating and taking part in family traditions. Encourage them to share their day's happenings during dinner. This boosts their self-esteem. And cuddling with them at bedtime creates a cozy and safe environment.

Think of the rituals you now enjoy. Together, plan one or two new rituals that will enhance the day and bring you closer.

II

How Do We Avoid Conflicts?

All couples have disagreements. Our goal is to understand why disagreements occur and what each of us is thinking during those periods of conflict. We can learn ways to seek solutions together rather than to cast blame.

The Blame Game

CINDY: Seth, I can't believe you didn't get better directions.

SETH: They said take a left on Spruce after the second light. They didn't mention the blinking light.

CINDY: And now it's raining, and we're going to miss the movie!

SETH: I bet you didn't bring umbrellas.

CINDY: We wouldn't need them if we were there on time. We go through this all the time. Why can't you ever get good directions? At least use the GPS. It works for me.

SETH: I can't trust those things. Don't you remember? Last time I used it, that woman's voice led me to a dead end in a warehouse area.

CINDY: Great, thanks to you the parking lot will be full. I'm really not interested in the movie anymore.

The Road to Power Snuggling

Blame becomes the autopilot that directs our stress toward each other. It can pervade our relationship for years. Blame may arise when we are lost on a rainy road, late for an appointment, or mishandling a checking account. The "Blame Game" stresses both players and delays a solution. Blame Games often involve countless, "If only you had . . ." phrases followed by "Yeah, but what about you?" How do we escape the Blame Game and interact in more productive ways?

Snuggling requires switching from the Blame Game to a new game, one that is much more fun and offers positive results with less stress: Solve and Resolve. In this game, players work as a team on the same side, as though they are completing a puzzle together. The game begins with the question, "What are we going to do now?" There should never be blame pinned on the other, even if we are sure it was our partner's fault.

In Solve and Resolve, Seth and Cindy's wrong turn might have sounded more like this:

SETH: I think we're lost. I thought this would be Spruce but it's Oak Street.

CINDY: Let me call and see if the box office can give us directions. If not, we'll look for a gas station.
SETH: I should have checked this out first. [It's okay to blame ourselves, but not our partner.]
CINDY: It's raining but I think we have some plastic in the trunk that will keep us dry. I'll check when we stop.

When Seth and Cindy play Solve and Resolve, they will be warm and dry in the theater after peacefully resolving the issue instead of missing the movie and working through the anger that exploded. They will feel relaxed and maybe hold hands. The next day they can calmly discuss how to avoid similar problems in the future. Easier said than done? Of course, change is not easy, but satisfying results can last a lifetime.

Sustaining Your Snuggle

How do you each react if something goes wrong and one of you is sure it is the other's fault? If there is blame, the usual response is fighting back with excuses and returning the blame, sparking a new confrontation. When you need to vent and let your partner know you are upset, give them an "I" message: "I'm upset that we might miss the movie." This approach states a fact without pointing a finger. Then you can use Solve and Resolve together to find a solution.

Think of instances when you played the Blame Game. Discuss ways you could have become closer by playing Solve and Resolve. Use this method the next time an issue arises.

Who Should Control the Purse Strings?

JACOB: How was I to know our checking account is low? You're the one who keeps track of our money. You should have told me. I have enough to do just bringing home most of the dough.

JENNY: I didn't know you were going to write such a large check. Just ask me first. You need to at least be somewhat aware of our financial status.

JACOB: Well, you never talk to me about what's going on. Whenever I ask you about our money you say, "I have it under control. IRAs and checkbooks are my responsibilities."

The Road to Power Snuggling

The phrase "controlling the purse strings" can be traced back to the fourteenth century when a family's wealth was kept in a purse filled with gold coins, held closed by tightly pulled strings. As it has been for centuries, control of a family's money continues to be a major issue. Whether we are trying to just make ends meet or put aside money to invest, conflicts will arise.

Olivia Mellan, author of *Money Harmony,* and Karina Piskaldo write in *Psychology Today*, "Spouses who start talking genuinely about what they like about each other's money style create an atmosphere of safety and non-defensiveness" ("Men, Women, and Money," January 1, 1999). They note that once we establish a way to discuss money issues and realize we each have a positive intent, we can find solutions to fit our unique needs.

Often couples assign one partner to manage most of the finances. One of us may take the lead, but both should have a say on spending and investing funds. We should discuss to what extent we will merge some, or all, of our common assets. For joint expenses, this is appropriate. However, we each should control at least some funds, particularly in our own checking account.

Solutions do not have to be entirely symmetrical, but they need to meet the needs of both partners. Invariably, some of us want to avoid thinking about balancing the budget or planning for the future, while others continually focus on these matters. As with many issues, the relationship benefits when we each use our unique abilities to meet family requirements.

Sustaining Your Snuggle

As soon as you set up house and begin to share money, establish a plan to control family funds. Just thinking, "We'll work it out" is never successful. Decide who is best suited to pay the bills and maintain records. The partner who wants to avoid money issues still needs to be regularly apprised of the financial status.

In case anything were to happen to your partner, you need to know the monthly budget, the location of your savings and investments, and how to access them. Agree on major purchases and plan ways to save and pay for them. Discuss money issues regularly.

What Bugs You?

Tom and Steve are talking at work.

TOM: Sandy is great most of the time, but what really bugs me is when she starts to file her nails in the car. Last week we're coasting along on the freeway. It was a beautiful spring day, and suddenly I hear this awful grating sound. It makes me cringe!

STEVE: That wouldn't bother me too much, but Marlene's making me wait while she takes her good ol' time bothers the heck outta me. She's all dressed, we're ready to leave, and she always—and I mean always—goes back into the house looking for something she forgot. Of course, guess who's waiting and fuming? I'm forced to sit waiting for her in a hot car.

That night, the men's wives, Sandy and Marlene, are talking on the phone.

SANDY: Tom is handy around the house, but it's so annoying when he walks in with muddy shoes and leaves his dirty tools on the furniture. I'm so over it, cleaning up after him. I've asked him not to do that dozens of times, but he either doesn't get it or just doesn't care. Then, of course, there's leaving the toilet seat up. That's a whole other issue.

MARLENE: Yeah, that is annoying. Steve's like that too. But what really ticks me off is when he slurps his soup. It may seem like a small thing, but it's disgusting to hear and embarrassing. Sometimes when we're out I see others looking at us. I'm sure they hear it. I tell him to control the noise. I mean, why can't he just eat quietly?

The Road to Power Snuggling

Annoying: The Science of What Bugs Us, by Joe Palca and Flora Lichtman, is a book describing how we all are irritated by some of the same things, such as a fly buzzing or nails screeching on a blackboard. In addition to these universal annoyances, we could each name specific behaviors that bug us individually. With relationships, these seemingly small problems can be abrasive and eventually cause major blowups.

So how do we de-bug? It is counterproductive to tell our partner, "Ninety-nine percent of people would have no problem with me leaving my sunglasses there" or "I bet if I took a poll, none of our neighbors would complain about me mowing the grass at eight in the morning." Instead, we need to listen to our partner's complaint and consider eliminating or altering the habit. Living as a couple requires us to make changes, often adjusting our ways to meet the other's needs.

Sustaining Your Snuggle

If some habits go unnoticed, like snapping your pen continuously, they won't hurt your relationship. But when either of you find a behavior too upsetting to ignore, follow this de-bugging guide.

If you are the perpetrator: First, stop the behavior. Be conscious of the slurp factor and try to eat the soup quietly. This may require waiting for it to cool. Second, engage in the offensive activity, such as filing your nails, when your partner is not present. Third, make corrections right away. For example, vacuum the floor immediately after you track in dirt. And don't forget that toilet seat.

Each partner should make a list of two or three behaviors that bug them, starting at the highest nuisance level. Give a head's up on how you intend to de-bug. Then do it! As has often been claimed, good habits are as hard to break as bad ones.

When Your Partner Won't Decide

STEVE: I'm not sure I wanna go. I may have other things going on.
LESLIE: You're kidding. You know the party's next week. The invitation came a month ago. I never thought you wouldn't go!
STEVE: They'll have enough food whether I go or not.
LESLIE: That's not the point. It's their special anniversary, so we need to let them know. You do this all the time. You can never make a simple decision. You're driving me crazy.
STEVE: You know that there might be an important game that afternoon or something else could come up . . .
LESLIE: I'm sick and tired of your stubbornness.

The Road to Power Snuggling

Couples often try to control each other in different ways. A common practice is delaying decisions, especially if the decision is high on their partner's wish list. Steve may eventually decide to go to the party, but not before using delaying tactics that help him feel he has some control.

Often children dawdle or disobey because they find it is a way to have some control in the family. Even if they are yelled at or punished, it is crucial for them to have some power. Maybe as a child, we had a controlling parent who insisted on getting their way with little compassion for our needs. In adulthood, when conflicts arise, we may find ways to maintain power by returning to childhood tactics.

Steve is likely to respond positively to Leslie if she finds ways to empower him. For instance, she can support his interests and ask for his opinions on various matters. As she considers his needs and reaches out, he will feel more valued and react positively. They will begin to reconnect.

Sustaining Your Snuggle

When your partner is delaying decisions, look behind the issue. Do they feel like they are an equal partner? Or do they think their opinions don't matter? Discuss, without accusation, what might be occurring. Of course, there are times when a decision has to be postponed. If so, your partner should clearly express their feelings and explain why the delay is necessary.

If your partner seems disinterested and aloof, they might be feeling unloved and unimportant. Support them in their endeavors and desires. Ask questions daily and listen attentively when they share their ideas and experiences. They will feel closer to you and in turn become more interested in your needs.

She Just Can't Take a Joke

A few days after the party, Fred spoke on the phone with his best friend, Justin.

JUSTIN: Your party was great. Everyone had a blast!
FRED: Yeah, it was fun. But now Elise is bummed out. She's hardly said a word to me in the last two days.
JUSTIN: Why?
FRED: She thought I made fun of her. I just don't get it. All I said was our kids would never have made the swim team if their physique was like hers. Okay, so I was jabbing her a little, but it's the truth. Is that so awful?
JUSTIN: Well, to be honest, I was kind of surprised by your comment.
FRED: Oh, come on, Justin. I just meant it to be a little joke. Why is everyone so sensitive? You know I didn't mean anything by it.

It makes no difference whether Fred's statement is true or not. Criticizing our partner in front of others can quickly deflate our relationship. People are often unaware of the impact a few words can have on their partner as well as others listening.

The Road to Power Snuggling

Our remarks might seem trivial when delivered, but they can damage a relationship for weeks. Consider the impact the following comments might have on those we love.

- Rosie never gets the punch line right. Let me tell you how it goes.
- You know how Bill can make a mountain out of a molehill? Well, he just did.
- Don't trust Sue to give you directions. She gets lost looking for the ladies' room.

Critical comments made in the presence of friends can be a not-so-subtle way of dealing with frustrations we have with our partner. If we are annoyed with them, we should save our observations for private times. If we need to offer constructive criticism, we should keep in mind a quote from American politician Frank A. Clark: "Criticism, like rain, should be gentle enough to nourish a man's growth without destroying his roots."

Sustaining Your Snuggle

The flip side of criticism is encouragement, which helps your partner grow. Positivity can be especially beneficial when you and your partner are in the presence of others. Complimenting your partner in a group is even more powerful than when you are alone. Reflect on the benefit of the following compliment: "Fran is very modest and won't boast, but she really outdid herself yesterday in her testimony before the county executive." Such praise communicates your pride in your partner, which enhances their feelings of connectedness to you. In our example, others will probably ask Fran follow-up questions, which will add more good feelings to this positive experience.

Discuss times when either of you felt hurt by critical comments one of you made in front of others. Talk about the impact this type of conversation has on everyone. Often, it leaves people feeling awkward and wondering who they should support or if they should just stay mum. Conversely, discuss times you each made uplifting comments about the other and how those comments affected you.

Support each other. The benefits will surprise you.

I Know What He's Thinking!

Melissa is talking on the phone to Leah.

MELISSA: So, as we drove, I casually mentioned Luigi's Italian restaurant. I said it would be perfect with the view of the water. But then David says, "How 'bout sushi?" So I say, "Sushi? Didn't we discuss Italian?" Then he says real loud, "You never said that." But I know I did and . . .

LEAH: Sushi can be good sometimes.

MELISSA: Yeah, but do you know why he said sushi? It was so obvious. In his own obnoxious way, he was telling me I'm gaining weight and he was pushing sushi because it has less calories. Is that being manipulative or what?

LEAH: Ouch! Then what happened?

MELISSA: Of course we had a big fight, and we went home. I found leftovers for myself. I have no idea what he had, and I couldn't care less!

The Road to Power Snuggling

Melissa doesn't think to herself, "David wants sushi; I want Italian. Let's discuss the options." Instead, she is sure David is trying to control her through her diet because she herself is insecure about her weight gain. What Melissa is experiencing is psychological projection. This occurs when a person unconsciously denies their own thoughts and instead ascribes those thoughts to others, believing the other originated the thoughts. David may have thought about calories when he suggested sushi. Or he may have had a yen for sushi without one thought about Melissa's weight. But she is convinced that David was referring to her weight gain. She is transferring her own uncomfortable thoughts to David.

When we are close with our partner, we are able to acknowledge our own inadequacies. We share our innermost thoughts and secrets, knowing our partner will support us. But when our relationship is weak, we feel vulnerable and tend to blame our partner for our own problems.

Sustaining Your Snuggle

Snuggling requires that you recognize when you are transferring your thoughts and attributing them to your partner. Recall when your partner made a comment that offended you. How did you react? Rethink their possible intention. Maybe their remark was unkind and it should never have been uttered. But perhaps it was meant to be taken at face value without other interpretations. When a comment like David's stirs controversy, focus on the suggestion or thoughts without seeking to interpret its potential underlying meanings.

Think about times when comments were blown out of proportion. Discuss how you both can become more conscious of your sensitivities when you feel threatened. Sharing these thoughts and reactions will lead to greater understanding and trust.

Waiting for the Marshmallow

Scott arrives home carrying his laptop, shoulders slumped. Amber can't wait, and she deals out her day: "It's been just miserable. First, Luke said his throat was sore, and he couldn't go to school but after a half-hour of moaning he said he was feeling better, so I drove him, and I was late for work. The electrician came while I was driving to school so we still have no lights in the basement. And after that it just got worse."

But Scott doesn't want to listen. He rolls his eyes, gives Amber a faint kiss on her cheek, and says he needs to unwind. He wanders into the bedroom. She glares at him. "You never want to hear about my day. I couldn't wait 'til you got home, and you . . ." But the bedroom door is already shut. She drops her jaw.

At dinner, they discuss Luke's grades and the traffic. They ignore their matching frowns.

The Road to Power Snuggling

In 1968, Dr. Walter Mischel conducted a landmark experiment at Stanford University. He placed a single marshmallow on a table in front of a four year old and told the child that if they did not eat the marshmallow, they would receive a second marshmallow when he returned to the room. He left for twenty minutes.

Dr. Mischel followed the lives of the children in the experiment. Years later, he found that those who had waited for the second marshmallow averaged an astounding 210 points higher on the Scholastic Aptitude Test (SAT) compared to the children who could not wait and had eaten the single marshmallow. The simple marshmallow test was twice as valid as IQ tests in predicting SAT scores. Following the participants over many years, Dr. Mischel also found that those who had waited for the second marshmallow had better high school and college grades, greater social competence, and less drug use.

The marshmallow experiment shows that patience, timing, and self-control have an enormous impact on accomplishments. Following this pattern, couples who develop the patience exhibited by these children will be much more likely to enjoy a mutual, long-lasting love relationship.

Amber needed to learn to wait for the second marshmallow. Eventually she was able to refrain from talking about her day or bombarding Scott with questions until he was ready. One evening she greeted him at the door, gave him a hug, and searched his eyes. He smiled and said he was tired. She asked, "Do you need anything?" He shook his head. She patted him on the shoulder as he went into the bedroom to rest. Later he came into the living room and turned on music. They held hands and talked, exchanging their day's happenings. On days when Scott felt calmer after work, he was able to listen to Amber's travails as soon as he arrived home. On days when Amber worked and Scott stayed home with the children, he too learned to give Amber time to regroup.

Sustaining Your Snuggle

Has anything ever bothered you so much that you could not imagine waiting another minute to share it with your partner? Although you may feel it is absolutely necessary to greet your partner with your day's problems, on-the-spot bombardment of an issue makes it difficult for them to support you. Aside from an emergency, consider your partner's frame of mind beforehand. You will get more mileage. Check their body language before you begin a discussion. If they are not listening, plan to hold your conversation later. Waiting for the second marshmallow raises your "Love SATisfaction."

How Arguments Evolve and How to Avoid Them

NICOLE: Turn off the computer and come fix the chair! You said you'd fix it last week.

JOSH: I work hard all week in the office, and I cut the grass yesterday. I just want to enjoy some of Saturday and figure out our baseball team's averages.

NICOLE: I go to work all week too and I buy the kids' clothes, cook the meals, make sure everything is on our schedule, and—

JOSH: Well, let's make a list of what needs to be done and when we can do it. I'll put it on a spreadsheet and check off each item.

NICOLE: All I want is for you to fix the freakin' chair!

JOSH: Hold on, I have to make a phone call.

The Road to Power Snuggling

The renowned family psychotherapist Virginia Satir wrote that we all use one or more of these four toxic communication styles during arguments:

- Blamer. The Blamer's philosophy is that the best defense is a good offense. They use loud, authoritative voices: "It's all your fault! If it weren't for you, everything would be fine."
- Placater. The Placater attempts to make you feel sorry for them so you will fill their needs. They may use a whiny voice: "You think I can't do anything right. I do more work than anyone, and no one appreciates it."
- Super Analyzer. The Super Analyzer resists showing you their feelings so that you cannot hurt them. They use a robotic voice: "I have it all figured out. You just need to . . . and then you should . . . and then you have to . . ."
- Distractor. The Distractor avoids the problem at all costs, hoping it will go away. They use a quiet, out-to-lunch voice: "Problem? What problem? I have to make a phone call."

These communication styles may feel right in the short term, but they harm your relationship in the long run. Using these poor styles of communication, arguments escalate as each person tries to strengthen their position. Can you identify the communication styles used between Nicole and Josh in the introductory narrative?

To avoid arguments, we should work together to solve problems rather than working against each other. Instead of the four negative approaches to communication illustrated by Josh and Nicole, use what Virginia Satir calls the Leveling Style. When we are a leveler, we respond to situations harmoniously. Our relationship feels easy, free, and honest. A leveler admits to their mistakes and apologizes. A leveler conducts life with integrity, commitment, and creativity. If we hear an apology, we should accept it. Satir notes that when we start to level, we will find our hearts. We will have a discussion rather than an argument. We will understand and forgive.

Nicole wants Josh to understand that the broken chair bothers her. Josh wants Nicole to understand that he needs to enjoy some of his weekend pleasures. They each would like the other to appreciate their hard work at the office and at home. They could try leveling:

NICOLE: Josh, the dining-room chair is still broken, and I'm afraid it will collapse if we continue to sit on it. Would you please fix it?

JOSH: You're right; it needs fixing. I'm trying to figure out our baseball team's averages. I'll find a time for the chair before the end of the day.

NICOLE: I know it's important for you to work on the team's averages. Thanks in advance for fixing the chair.

Sustaining Your Snuggle

Be conscious when you are using any of Satir's four negative communication styles. Seek to change the conversation from adversarial to compromising. Use the Leveling Style, and you will enjoy peaceful and heartfelt conversations, avoiding the angst of battling.

Avoiding "Exits" in Your Relationship

SHARON: You're running out again? You've already played golf this week.

JERRY: I told you last week that we have that special tournament today.

SHARON: So here I am, stuck with the household chores, the kids, and the air-conditioner guy. You're always with your friends playing golf. When you're not playing golf, you're holed up in your office on the computer for hours. What happened to our together time? Remember when we'd go biking together? Remember when we'd enjoy a night out at the theater?

JERRY: Look, Sharon, you know how important golf is to me. I've been playing all my life. Are you asking me to quit something I love? I can't imagine life without golf. As for my time on the computer, you're greatly exaggerating.

SHARON: Our friends make time to do things together. They all have jobs and kids, but they make time to have fun together. With us, it's nonexistent. I'm sick and tired of feeling lonely!

The Road to Power Snuggling

We all need some space in our relationship. We usually work in separate locations and have our own friends, hobbies, chores, and pleasures. It is a tricky balance to maintain personal interests and yet stay emotionally connected. Without that connection, we may attempt to distance ourselves and seek "exits" from our relationship.

What is an exit? Time apart becomes an exit when unresolved conflicts and resentment cause us to feel so uncomfortable that we need to get away. We seek ways to replace stressful home situations with more pleasurable activities. Exits can be continually working extra-long hours, spending considerable time with our individual friends, excessive reading, constantly talking on the phone, an unreasonable amount of time spent watching or playing sports, frequently staying on the computer, or continual involvement with the children, leaving little time or energy for our partner.

When do exits become too much? In moderation separate activities are necessary; we all need time alone for our individual activities. But if our partner feels they are last on the totem pole, then beware! The situation can result in an emotional downward spiral, possibly followed by an affair, separation, and divorce.

How do we prevent exits? Snuggling can be recaptured if we work toward, and maintain, an open line of communication. We need to be available for our partner emotionally. When they are experiencing difficulties, we should be there for them and listen with sensitivity. We give them a gift when they express themselves to us without being judged. If their problems involve us, we should listen and validate their concerns. And they need to listen and validate us as well. There may be no quick resolution; however, we have begun a process of sharing thoughts.

We should also show an interest in each other's activities. We can look for mutually enjoyable pastimes as a way of connecting.

Sustaining Your Snuggle

How much time do you and your partner spend together? Are you allocating time for each other every day? Do you keep them apprised of daily events and stay in the loop yourself? You may need to juggle or eliminate some activities to remain connected.

Check in with your partner as to why they are not spending time with you. Listen, without interruption, to their comments and maintain open and friendly communication. Make regular plans for a day or nighttime date, with some imaginative outings just for fun.

You Have Power. Use it!

As Carl drives home from work, his belly aches and his head whirls: "This is too, too much! I work. Kelly works. Sometimes we even have to work overtime. We're constantly caring for our two daughters, plus carrying out our daily chores. I'm sure some of our friction results from our busy schedules, with little time for fun. We need to make time for us. Maybe we can get a babysitter on Fridays and have a date night. Then at least once a week we'll relax together."

After Carl arrives home, he tells Kelly what he's been thinking. She loves the idea and immediately schedules a babysitter. All week, Carl and Kelly look forward to their date night.

When Friday comes, they have a great time at an outdoor concert, followed by a light snack. Just getting away and reigniting that bond between them brings a new perspective to their humdrum life. They decide to continue planning dates for Friday nights.

The Road to Power Snuggling

We may love many aspects of our relationship. We remember happy times, and we visualize lovely moments: leisurely talking, holding hands, eating out, and perhaps hitting the dance floor. But something is missing, and there are always conflicts waiting to be resolved. We think, "Wouldn't it be great if we could improve some areas of our relationship that aren't working? Wouldn't it be great if we could live with less friction?"

Understanding the process of purposeful change will help us take positive action in redirecting the course of our relationship. It is a three-pronged process, which we can view as the ABCs of change:

Affect: Our emotions and feelings.
Behavior: The actions we take.
Cognition: How we think about issues.

When we alter just one of these ABCs, the other two will frequently follow suit.

In Carl's situation, the process begins with his emotional response.

Affect:	He felt, "I'm tired and overwhelmed. It's causing physical problems. There's too much work, too many home duties, and no relaxation—just friction."
Cognition:	He thought, "We need a change. We should get a babysitter, and plan on a date night every Friday."
Behavior:	He acted: he spoke with Kelly, who in turn scheduled a babysitter.

For Carl and Kelly the process continued with another emotional change that reinforced the positive cycle they had started: they were elated and had such a wonderful time that they made plans for the following Friday.

This process can also begin with a behavior.

Behavior:	At the office, Carl donated money to a charity. As a thank-you, the charity sent a small bouquet of flowers to his office. He brought the flowers home to Kelly.
Affect:	Kelly was thrilled, which pleased Carl.
Cognition:	Carl realized how much the flowers meant to Kelly, so he made a mental note to bring her flowers more often.

The three processes may begin at any point, A, B, or C. In the first scenario, Carl began with the Affect, or A, approach. In the second scenario, he began the process with the Behavior, or B, approach. We have the power to change situations by using any combination of these processes. These tools will improve our relationship and our lifestyle. Without taking the risk of trying something new, we are bound by the status quo.

Sustaining Your Snuggle

What aspects of your relationship would you like to change? Using the Affect, Behavior, Cognitive interaction, jot down your plan in the appropriate categories.

Imagine how your life together will become more conscious and energized as you use these tools to bring about positive change. In a conscious relationship, we express ourselves openly with our partner, always being aware of their needs and comfort level. We listen to them, caring deeply about what they think and feel, and we respect their individuality. Our hearts are open, and we are consistently honest. In a conscious relationship, we are friends through thick and thin.

III

The Power of the Past

In relationships, our past and our partner's past are continually meeting. To understand what is occurring in the present, we often have to search yesterday's experiences.

The Orange

She spoke as if she were reliving her childhood experience: "I was so, so embarrassed. Daddy said to go to Frank's Grocery and pick him up an orange. So, quick like a bunny, I was running down that dusty dirt road near Billings Pig Farm, where the smell drifted into my nostrils, and headed for Frank's. I spread the six pennies on the counter and ran all the way home squeezing the orange to my chest, a few chickens fluttering by. Felt smart too when I handed Daddy the orange. He smiled, but I knew he was upset: 'I meant an orange pop to drink, not an orange to eat.' He laughed and gave me a hug, but I felt like falling right through the floor. I really did."

Glenda (not her real name) was 92 years old when we visited her in a nursing home. She confided that for 85 years she was too embarrassed to tell that story to anyone.

The Road to Power Snuggling

If we take the time to recall a powerful memory, we enter the past and re-experience the scene we left decades ago. We see people's faces, hear the sounds, and even smell the day. We delve into the limbic portion of our brain, which has no sense of time. The past feels like the present. The evolutionary purpose for recalling these scenes is to arm ourselves against perceived new dangers. Thus, a small remark might trigger an old memory and cause an emotional avalanche, even if the potential threat our brain detects is not a real danger.

If one grows up in an alcoholic household, hearing a joke about liquor can evoke major anger. A sexual innuendo heard by a sexual abuse victim can wreak havoc. And yes, Glenda may find that she dislikes a man in her nursing home when she sees him drink an orange soda, but she is unlikely to understand why.

Sustaining Your Snuggle

When you find that anger or sadness is blown out of proportion, an uncomfortable memory may have been exposed. Over time, you will learn what comments trigger these emotions.

Think of a disagreement you and your partner have experienced. Capture your emotion triggered by that situation. Then think of a childhood experience when you felt a similar emotion (though not necessarily in a similar situation). It is much healthier to share this discovery than to repress it. Recalling and sharing childhood events provides a framework for mutual understanding and trust.

Messages from Your First Love

Do you recall when you first had a crush on that boy or girl and could think of nothing else? Remember waking up and visualizing their face, hearing their voice, and continuing the romance in your mind's eye? Remember pretending to hear them say, "I love you"? Even now you may think, "If only I had married that perfect person."

James Joyce's short story "The Dead" (later a movie) tells of a woman whose first love died as a teenager. The woman's husband realizes that she is still thinking of her lost beau and idealizing the life she would have led had she married him. No matter how much her husband tries, he finds he cannot compete with his wife's image of her lost love.

The Road to Power Snuggling

At times we might compare our partner to lost loves, others we meet, or even to movie stars. The romance of short-term glimpses may seem perfect compared to our everyday lives. Dr. Gayle Brewer, a lecturer in social psychology at the University of Central Lancashire, agrees. "If you judge adult relationships against your first relationship, you are using a single benchmark: that of an intense and unrealistic passion," she says. "Adult relationships need all sorts of other virtues to survive, many of which are not compatible with that level of intensity" (Amelia Hill, "Why We Can Never Recover from First Love," TheGuardian.com/us, January 17, 2009). All relationships evolve from that initial romantic force to the necessity of dealing with practical situations. Real life is a combination of beauty and romance mixed with preparing meals, paying bills, and fighting traffic. If we seek perfection, we will always be disappointed.

Sustaining Your Snuggle

When you struggle with some of life's disappointments, you may think of past times that seemed easier, more exciting, and more loving. Reminiscing can be therapeutic and comforting. However, if you dwell on the good old days, it becomes difficult to live fully in the present.

You cannot ignore these memories since your life is built on them. As they float into your mind, remember that they often include an unrealistic glow of what was and what could have been. It is useful to share these memories. Each of you will have both pleasant and unpleasant memories of your lives before you met each other. Sharing memories will help you better understand each other and bring you closer together.

It is also useful to recall the time you fell in love with your partner. Remember the laughs, the flirting, and the natural feeling of give-and-take? Think of the meaningful times you have shared over the years. Work toward recapturing that romance.

Emotional Allergies

Mary and Tom have finished dinner and they are leaving the restaurant.

MARY: That was lovely. The food was delicious, and the waitress was really nice. She brought all the food to us right away.

TOM: Yep. And she was pretty. She also had a great figure.

MARY: What does that have to do with anything?

TOM: What do you mean? All I said was, "She was pretty and had a great figure."

MARY: So, I'm not pretty with a great figure? Tom! How do you think that makes me feel?

TOM: Look, I'm sorry about whatever I said that caused you to totally overreact. I didn't say anything bad about you.

MARY: Yeah, right. But I know what you meant. Let's forget about going to the movie.

TOM: Why? You wanted to see it. It got great reviews and—

MARY: I've had enough! I want to go home.

The Road to Power Snuggling

In every love relationship, conflicts arise because what one person believes is a trivial comment hurts the other to the core. Tom and Mary's conversation illustrates a common gender difference in sexual thoughts and importance of body image. These powerful reactions are often caused by "emotional allergies." Similar to a physical allergy, an emotional allergy might mean a high sensitivity to an issue due to prior experiences.

When Mary was in her teens, she became increasingly aware that her father had a roving eye. He would frequently stare at passing women. Then she heard her mother's angry words. She also recalls feeling creepy when her father quickly covered the screen of his smart phone and turned away from her. Over the years she has shared those uncomfortable incidents with Tom, who has also been witness to the consequences of her discomfort.

We are all sensitive to some topics because of our history, which continues to impact our current relationship. Based on Mary's history, and prior reactions, Tom's comment was unfortunate and insensitive. He should have known how Mary would feel. Over time, relationships succeed as each understands—and avoids—behaviors that can upset the other.

Sometimes, we hear partners defend themselves with, "Yeah, but I hate walking on eggshells. I need to be myself and speak my mind." Yes, we need to be ourselves, but we also need to understand our partner's limits. We don't walk up to a friend and say, "Gee, you've aged!" A warm relationship requires that we respect our partner as we would a good friend.

Sustaining Your Snuggle

Be mindful of emotional allergies. In a conscious relationship, you need to be aware of each other's sensitivities. Sharing past experiences provides valuable information that leads to better understanding: you avoid having to guess what your partner is feeling.

Think before you make comments that might cause an emotional avalanche. Ask yourself, "Will this trigger something hurtful in my partner and damage our relationship?"

If your partner's remarks set off one of your emotional allergies, explain your feelings and experiences rather than reacting harshly.

Admit it. You're Criticizing Me!

Alexia's mother is visiting. The two women are in the kitchen preparing a meal together.

MOTHER: So you're putting parsley flakes on the rice?

ALEXIA: What's so wrong with parsley flakes?

MOTHER: Nothing. I didn't say anything is wrong. But I've never put parsley on rice, and I've never seen it done before.

ALEXIA: Mom, will you ever stop criticizing me?

MOTHER: Alexia, I was just stating the fact that I saw you put parsley on the rice. So where does criticism come into this? I was only making conversation.

ALEXIA: Mom! Admit it, you don't think I can cook as well as you, so you're letting me know that there's a better way and that I shouldn't put parsley flakes on the rice. Well, I happen to think it looks good, and it definitely makes the rice taste better.

MOTHER: Oh, Alexia, stop being so ridiculous. I can't seem to open my mouth without you finding a reason to get angry with me. (*She throws her apron on the floor and stomps out of the room.*)

The Road to Power Snuggling

Whether we are speaking with our mother, a friend, or our partner, we regularly hear metamessages. Dr. Deborah Tannen, a professor of linguistics at Georgetown University and author of *That's Not What I Meant!*, conducted extensive research on the way people talk to each other and emphasizes that people regularly use metamessages to disguise the true meaning of their comments. *Meta* is from the Greek, meaning "after" or "beyond." A metamessage, then, is a message that has an underlying meaning beyond the face value of the words. Seeking the coded meaning, people commonly misconstrue a message thinking that it is intended to be critical. Since couples and family members have years of shared experience, seemingly innocent words or actions can echo uncomfortable previous occurrences and trigger strong emotions. For example, Alexia and her mother have a history of quibbling back and forth about the best way to accomplish a task. In the kitchen scene, Alexia feels attacked by her mother due to her memories of past faultfinding. If someone else had spoken the same words, Alexia may have taken the words as friendly conversation or even a compliment.

To avoid conflicts, we need to limit our use of metamessages and restrain our emotions when we feel criticized. If we immediately react, we may prompt a long-lasting argument. Later we may wonder, "Why did that remark hit me so hard?" By understanding that these apparently innocuous statements are triggers that reach back in our relationship history, we can control our reactions and avoid unnecessary conflict.

Sustaining Your Snuggle

Think of statements either of you have made that bore a hint of criticism. How did you respond in those situations? Sensitivities do not disappear easily since they are a part of your history together. If you comment on something in an ambiguous way with a metamessage, it can be more harmful to your relationship than a direct hit. Your partner will feel you are being manipulative. When the timing is right, use "I" messages to respond to hurtful comments directed at you. Using "I" messages, Alexia and her mother's conversation could have ended differently:

MOTHER: I feel bad that I upset you. I didn't mean to.
ALEXIA: I felt I was being criticized and that my way of doing things is never good enough.

Listen and refrain from arguing over "I" messages. They describe emotions, and you are both entitled to your feelings. Validate each other's feelings, even when you don't agree. Sometimes you may need to bite your tongue, allowing you time to regroup and find a more effective way to handle the situation.

Mom, Marriage Isn't What I Expected

Shortly after her fifth wedding anniversary, Lisa flies to Arizona to visit her mother. As they sit outside, enjoying a cup of coffee, the conversation shifts to a discussion about Lisa's marriage.

MOM: So you and Brian have been together for five years now. How's marriage treating you?

LISA: Oh, it's okay. But not like I expected.

MOM: No?

LISA: Well, Brian and I were so much in love. I thought everything would always be just wonderful. Not perfect, because I know marriage has its ups and downs, but I thought that most days would be romantic. You know, like what you and Dad had.

MOM: And it's not?

LISA: I thought we'd go out dancing like you and Dad. And Brian would make a lot of money like Dad. I thought Brian would at least remember Valentine's Day like when Dad brought you flowers.

MOM: That's not Brian?

LISA: Don't get me wrong. Brian can be a caring guy. We go to movies and enjoy our kids and friends. We even decorated our house together. But dullness has set in. The romance comes and goes. It's not like it used to be.

MOM: You know, it wasn't perfect with Dad either. He would blow up over little things. And he was always working late and missing family meals. We would also bicker about little things.

LISA: I guess I forgot about all that.

MOM: So you thought marriage means you'd have only the good things Dad and I had, but none of the bad?

LISA: I guess so. I thought every day would be romantic regardless of day-to-day problems.

MOM: That sounds like a Hollywood movie. When you first meet, you feel that most things are perfect, and anything that isn't, you can fix. The earth-shattering, falling-in-love romance that you had at first can't last forever. That would be exhausting!

For Dad and me, understanding each other's point of view was key, like when we had big disagreements. It was a challenge, but it grew easier. We decided it was important to tell each other every day how much we appreciated each other. Over time, our love grew much deeper than the love we had when we first met. Our reward was more trust and intimacy.

The Road to Power Snuggling

Long-term love is more subdued than storybook romance, but it is much deeper and more satisfying. After visiting her mother, Lisa began to realize that continual romantic love is the imagined ideal, not a realistic goal. She was focusing on what worked well in her parents' marriage rather than recognizing what worked in her own marriage and appreciating Brian's dependable and caring ways. Unrealistic expectations lead to disappointments. A successful marriage requires valuing what works with a positive and realistic expectation of what is possible.

Sustaining Your Snuggle

How do you react when your partner does not provide you with the loving behaviors you desire? Do you become sullen and aloof? Or do you search for more subtle ways they demonstrate their love?

When you have specific needs, calmly ask for what you want. You cannot expect your partner to know your desires if you are silent. It is also important to ask them to share their own desires.

Marriage is not about daily heartthrob romance. Rather, marriage is a revelation of long-term love that is built on accepting parts of your partner that are not likely to change while discovering behaviors that will please you both.

Money, Money, Money

They are into it again, arguing over money:

PAM: You know, I'm really tired of being so careful every time I want to mention spending money. Both of us work hard and make good salaries. I shouldn't have to feel so lousy about buying something I need. It's not like I'm a spendthrift.
SHANE: Okay, Pam, so what are you getting at?
PAM: See, that's what I mean. You immediately get defensive.
SHANE: I get it. You've already bought it, right?
PAM: Bought what? Even if I did, it's hard to enjoy a purchase that I know I need when it becomes more about your stubborn attitude!
SHANE: I give up. Obviously, I have no say in our finances.

The Road to Power Snuggling

Of all the subjects that couples discuss, money is perhaps the most challenging. A 2014 survey by Marketing & Research Resources found that about 70 percent of couples argue regularly over money issues, ahead of arguments over household chores, sex, togetherness, and snoring. This percentage only drops when couples are over 65 years old, and even then 60 percent of couples are still arguing over money. Everyday we have money on our minds, as we worry about bills or tell each other what we have purchased or are about to purchase. Money arguments involve much more than how to spend and save. While talking about finances, we are unconsciously thinking about our security, our love, and our power.

We need to communicate so that our conflicts will be handled maturely, without harming or completely altering our relationship. If we are emotionally close, it is much easier to work on financial issues and understand how our partner thinks about money. However, if we have conflicts in other areas and already feel resentful, we might even find ourselves purchasing items to annoy our partner.

Sustaining Your Snuggle

Childhood messages from parents regarding money can have a major impact on your current financial values. Discuss these questions with your partner:

- What messages did you receive from your parents regarding money?
- How have these messages influenced the way you now think and act regarding money?
- What are your fears with respect to spending or saving?

How does your partner react toward your spending and saving ideas, and how do you react toward theirs? Schedule regular times to discuss finances. Set individual goals as well as short-term and long-term family goals. Listen to both sides of the issues and validate each other, moving toward a mutual understanding.

Jon and Beverly's Argument

The following incident occurred a number of years ago. A new high-end furniture store was about to open in our neighborhood. The sign read, "Coming Soon! Visit us Saturday for Grand Opening!" Early Friday evening, we walked by the store and spotted a crowd inside.

JON: Let's stop in and take a look at the furniture. There are people coming out with silver goody bags.

BEVERLY: But they're all dressed up. We're in our shorts. We can't go in there like this.

JON: They don't care. They want to sell their furniture.

(*Jon enters and walks quickly towards the center of the store. Beverly, hesitating, is stopped at the door.*)

MAN: May I help you, Miss? What is your name?

BEVERLY: Beverly.

MAN, *looking at his clipboard*: Hmmm. I don't see any "Beverly." This is an invitation-only, pre-opening party. The store officially opens tomorrow.

BEVERLY: My husband's already inside. I'd better get him.

(*With some difficulty, Beverly eases Jon out of the crowded store, sans goody bag.*)

BEVERLY, *walking home*: I'm so embarrassed. What makes you think you can just barge in? This is a fancy, invitation-only party. Most people are wearing tuxes! (*Beverly recalls the words of her mother: "Society's rules are rules. You'll get in trouble if you break them!" She remembers being nine years old and very embarrassed, coming out of her room wearing pajamas while her parents were having a party.*) I think rules should be followed. You just can't ignore them.

JON: What's the big deal? It's a furniture store. They want people to see and buy their furniture. (*Jon remembers his mother's praise: "You're so adventurous and creative. You'll try anything. You'll go far!"*) To live fully, sometimes you have to do something that's unconventional. You can't always follow rules.

The Road to Power Snuggling

At home, we discussed what had occurred at the furniture store. We talked about the parental messages that supported each of our actions. Of course, we both felt we were right. But as we talked, we realized it made sense that the other would act in a way that was consistent with their childhood messages. Our actions would have been reversed if we had been born into the other's family. There is no right or wrong way to act in these circumstances. However, when we relate this story to couples, they usually pick a side based on their own upbringing.

Many couples' arguments result from differing values that develop in childhood. These values tend to be held forever. Even though values differ, discussing why and reaching back to their roots helps us understand both points of view.

Sustaining Your Snuggle

Do you recall arguments you have had as a result of your differing childhood messages? Recognize that your backgrounds play a significant role in your lives, and differences will surface, particularly when you have a disagreement. Can you see how your opinions would be different if you had each grown up in the other's family? Discuss these possibilities to help understand how arguments arise and to ease future conflicts.

Talk about a situation when you couldn't see eye-to-eye, and you were both adamant about your positions. Then discuss how those positions were influenced by childhood messages.

IV

Why Do We Argue over Loading the Dishwasher?
& Other Stuff
♥ ♥ ♥ ♥ ♥

Our disagreements often involve the stuff of our lives, such as what we should or should not buy or the best way to load the dishwasher. However, behind these squabbles is really something much deeper: Does my partner respect my values and abilities? Does my partner really love me?

If we feel our character and ideas are respected, there is greater harmony. When love is strong, we understand that we each have our unique talents and individual methods for accomplishing tasks. When love is strong, we do not feel as though we must compete. Instead, we work together to resolve problems.

Why Do We Argue over Loading the Dishwasher?

KEVIN: Make sure you line up the glasses in the dishwasher. That way, you'll get more in and save water.

CHRISTIE: I have more important things to think about than squeezing in every last thing.

KEVIN: Watch. It just takes a second, and the dishes get cleaner. See? And make sure the plates face the front of—

(*Christie slams the dishwasher door and stomps off.*)

KEVIN, *yelling after her*: What's wrong? I just thought I'd help you learn how to do it right.

CHRISTIE, *from the next room*: Gimme a break! I can figure out how to load the damn dishwasher.

After Kevin and Christie calm down, they may ask themselves, "What was that all about? Why did such a silly thing have to turn into a major conflict?"

The Road to Power Snuggling

What is happening with Kevin and Christie is common with couples. Each believes they are right. They are both correct, but their goals are different. He tries to be efficient by slipping in the last fork. And while she's dealing with the kids, she is satisfied loading the dishwasher any way she can. Their issue, however, has nothing to do with loading the dishwasher. It is a power struggle in which neither partner wants to accept the other's values.

Kevin and Christie are speaking to each other using the analytical part of their brains. They each know that their position makes the most sense for them. But it is the powerful, emotional part of their brain, housed in the brain's limbic system, that tells them, "Uh-oh. This is dangerous. My partner's trying to control me again, and my needs are being completely ignored."

Being in control of our life is essential to all of us. This is a basic right that we learn in early childhood. We fear we will lose part of ourselves when we are told how to do something that we know we can do.

Sustaining Your Snuggle

What is the solution? First, understand the issue. It is not an analytical problem about the best way to load the dishwasher. Rather, it is emotionally charged, involving who is controlling whom. Second, acknowledge each other's desires. For Christie and Kevin, the conversation could go something like this:

> CHRISTIE: Kevin, I know you want to save energy and have clean dishes.
> KEVIN: I know you have other things on your mind, so you're looking for the quickest way to get the job done.

Third, find a solution that allows both of you to feel in control. This might mean agreeing that the person loading the dishes does it their way. Family labor might be divided so one person cooks and the other washes dishes and cleans up. Relationships are too valuable to destroy over how to load the dishwasher.

Company's Coming!

JESSICA: The whole family's coming. There'll be over a dozen people, so we have to get things in order.

GARY: Get ready now? They're coming on Saturday. This is only Wednesday.

JESSICA: Yes, now. You always want to wait 'til the last minute. We have to make sure we have coals for the grill, make ice cubes, buy wine, and get out serving dishes and silverware. I have to straighten the shades, put things away, and set the dining room table soon. We can't wait until the last minute. It would be a disaster!

GARY: Huh? You have to set the table? They are coming in three days. There's plenty of time to do all that. We can't keep eating every meal in our tiny kitchen this week. It takes one minute to flop the plates on the table.

JESSICA: Gary! You don't just "flop" plates down. I have to make sure the design is facing where the person sits. Your grandfather needs a comfortable chair, the kids need booster seats, and you . . . You have no idea what it takes to plan a party. You'll be away at the computer store all week looking at gadgets while I'm slaving to prepare. I know what'll happen. You'll decide to take a shower twenty minutes before everyone arrives and then show up like you're the guest of honor.

GARY: Look, I don't want you to be stressed, but I think it's way too early. Fine, what do you want me to do?

JESSICA: Forget it. If I have to tell you each little thing, it's easier to do it myself.

The Road to Power Snuggling

In 1962, Katharine Cook Briggs and her daughter, Isabel Briggs Myers, expanded on Carl Jung's 1921 book *Psychological Types* to develop the Myers-Briggs Type Indicator (MBTI). The MBTI measures how people perceive the world differently and behave accordingly. Part of the Myers-Briggs indicator compares the planning-ahead type of person versus the delaying type.

According to the MBTI, the Planner likes to look at details, targets, and dates. They then finish chores in meaningful, step-by-step segments. They get anxious when decisions are delayed and deadlines are near. The Planner wants to have standard routines they can count on. They are goal-oriented.

The Delayer, in contrast, is laid-back with time pressures; they enjoy multi-tasking to meet the deadlines. They are energized with the freedom and flexibility in delaying. They are willing to bend as situations change. The Delayer likes a mix of work and play and thrives on new adventures to stimulate their life.

Jessica and Gary see the world through two different processes. This is not unusual. Many of us select a partner who has the opposite take on accomplishing a task. We unconsciously know that we can benefit from the other's methods, which often fill some of our shortcomings. Yes, Gary feels it is a waste of time to plan the party so early, but he also realizes that some preparation is needed. He knows from experience that Jessica is a good organizer, while organization is one of his weaknesses. Jessica knows that Gary is good at multi-tasking, and he eventually steps up to the plate. She also secretly admires the way he stays calm under pressure, which helps soothe her nerves.

Sustaining Your Snuggle

Appreciate your different styles of accomplishing tasks. Make a list of each of your strengths. Who naturally takes over and likes to plan ahead? Who takes the relaxed approach and is slower to the finish line? Don't keep tabs on who does more or less.

For the Planner, decide which tasks can be delegated and when they should be completed. Be flexible in getting the help you need. The best outcome is when you are pleased with your partner's help, and they feel useful. Over time, allow yourself to enjoy spur-of-the-moment activities that your Delayer partner suggests.

For the person who is more laid-back, appreciate your partner's planning skills and accept delegated tasks without resentment. Realize that your partner will become uptight if schedules are ignored. Stick to a reasonable time frame that will work for both of you. Together, you can use your talents to plan and prepare for success.

It's Not Really about Socks on the Floor

DIANA: Peter, you left your socks on the floor again. How many times do I have to remind you to put them in the hamper?
PETER: Jeez. I work all day and fall into bed exhausted. Then I have to deal with you worrying about socks you can't even see in the dark!
DIANA: I don't need to see them. I smell them with the other clothes you just dump. I really can't stand this anymore.
PETER: When I get home, I look forward to relaxing. I can't worry about stupid things like socks on the floor.
DIANA: Oh really? What about me? When do you think I have time to relax? Never! There's always something to do.

The Road to Power Snuggling

Many seemingly small issues lead to Power Struggles. When anger erupts, it is not really about socks on the floor, wet sponges left in the sink, or missing toothpaste caps. Behind all anger are hurt feelings, and behind the hurt feelings is a belief that we are not being listened to, that we are not being understood or appreciated. We feel invisible. We are convinced our partner does not care about us and we feel unimportant. We all need to feel heard, and we need to believe that our partner cares. If either of us is emotionally unavailable, the relationship will go downhill.

Diana and Peter need a two-way, nonabrasive connection. If they were feeling closer, Diana may not have brought up the subject of socks on the floor. However, even connected couples can struggle with the trivial. It is how they communicate, without anger and with consideration for the other, that prevents the insignificant from becoming a roadblock to Power Snuggling. Diana could have framed her complaint about the socks this way: "Honey, I'd appreciate it if you would put your clothes in the hamper." With this request Peter has an out without feeling blamed and will more likely head for the hamper.

Diana's first approach shows disapproval and the second method shows respect. If we are shown that we are valued, we will overcome these situations instead of initiating battles.

Sustaining Your Snuggle

The key to Snuggling is connecting emotionally. This requires acknowledging when your behavior bothers your partner. Even if you believe what you did was trivial, your partner needs to know that you care about their feelings. When a dispute arises, restrain your anger and try validating your partner. Try using phrases such as "I understand this bothers you" or "I know how you feel about this."

Validating doesn't mean agreeing. It means you accept your love partner's feelings and are willing to discuss both sides of the issue. Once feelings are accepted as genuine, it will be easier to discuss the issue more calmly and rationally.

The Facebook Fiasco

SHANNON: Chad, you really didn't, did you?
CHAD: Really didn't what?
SHANNON: You know.
CHAD: I don't know what you're talking about.
SHANNON: Jessica said she saw a vacation photo of us on your Facebook page. You know, the one where I was wearing a bathing suit.
CHAD: Yeah, so?
SHANNON: So that was an awful picture. I looked like a huge flounder with a sunburn laying on the beach. You can't just post photos of me on Facebook without asking.
CHAD: Well, everyone posts vacation pics on Facebook. We were having fun. I was sunburned, too and—
SHANNON: I'm so humiliated! I can't believe you did this to me.

The Road to Power Snuggling

In healthy relationships, couples should share their thoughts and feelings with each other to promote closeness. However, the things we reveal to our partner are not always meant for the eyes and ears of others. Sometimes an item or thought is shared outside the relationship without regard to the other's feelings. This can impact our relationship by damaging our trust and harming that feeling of security we seek from a love relationship.

Today, the means of distribution and the speed of dissemination of our thoughts, feelings, and personal images is greater than ever, making our respect for our partner's privacy even more important. A few decades ago, personal photos and information were privately shared with friends. With Facebook, email, and Twitter circling the globe, personal information can be viewed anywhere by anyone. Before clicking "send," we need to discuss with our partner what we are willing to share with others. At a time before Facebook, Shannon could have stopped Chad from showing photos in their living room. Today, Chad and Shannon need to agree about what each feels is appropriate to communicate to the world.

Beyond what we share with those outside of our love relationship, even as a couple we are each entitled to a level of individual privacy. We are entitled to personal privacy when engaging in phone conversations, reading snail mail addressed personally to us, taking a moment of time alone for ourselves, or using the private spaces in our home. Everyone has a right to schedule their day with events and people to see without sharing that information if they so choose.

We may confuse privacy with secrecy. Generally it is best not to withhold secrets from our partner. Secrets complicate a close, intimate relationship, interfering with our emotional bonds. Of course, purchasing a gift or keeping something under wraps for a short time as a surprise is the exception.

Sustaining Your Snuggle

Have either of you ever shared something that was considered private? How did you each react? Make it a priority to respect each other's right to privacy both in person and online. Be respectful of your different views. You may feel it is okay to share your Facebook page with everyone. On the other hand, your partner might feel their privacy is being invaded if you disclose anything pertaining to them without their permission. Discuss information you are both willing to share. If in doubt, always ask.

Hold Hands, Not Handhelds

Sonia is on the phone with Isabel:

SONIA: Ethan will finally be home early tonight, and we can spend some time together. Wait, I'm getting a text message. It looks like he has to work late again.
ISABEL: That has to be so annoying.
SONIA: Now I'm getting a text from my son. He wants to make sure I have what he likes for dinner. Isabel, this never stops.
ISABEL: I know what you mean. I feel as if my family communicates solely through text message. Frank's rarely available for a real conversation. He's either hung up on emails, playing games, or checking scores. Then there's Facebook and Twitter.

The Road to Power Snuggling

New technology allows us to keep in touch in many ways. Mouse clicks may be efficient when keeping up with events, but they diminish rather than replace emotional connections. Arianna Huffington, publisher of *The Huffington Post,* writes in her book, *Thrive,* "Unfortunately the ever-increasing creep of technology—into our lives, our families, our bedroom, our brains—makes it much harder to renew ourselves. The average smartphone user checks his or her device every six and a half minutes" ([New York: Harmony, 2014], 50). Facebook, Twitter and countless emails are no substitute for talking around the table and discussing our day's events.

We can remember when we first met our partner and talked for hours while sipping a cup of coffee. We took the time to appreciate the beauty of each other's personality without interruption. Today's high-tech allows for small clips of togetherness but fosters little depth of feeling. Computer keystrokes lack emotion and leave us disconnected from one another.

Sustaining Your Snuggle

How do you return to those one-on-one, in-person times? You need not toss away your handhelds, but you can do what couples have done for thousands of years, before high-tech devices: reserve time to dine together, sans all disruptions. Yes, actually turn off all devices at dinnertime. Then you will hear each other's voices, see each other's facial expressions, and again experience the love connection you had while dating.

You may even dare to do what some families practice: ban smartphones from your vacations. Surprisingly, you will survive, and your relationship will be nurtured through long and loving conversations.

Regularly make time together, without electronics, a priority. Rediscover the warmth of a relaxing conversation to fully listen to each other. If you have children, use this opportunity to share thoughts and feelings. Hold hands instead of handhelds.

How Can Such a Little Remark Wreak Havoc?

Dan and Denise are dining in a small local restaurant.

DENISE: You like my new blouse?
DAN: Yes, it's very pretty. I see it has a Polo label.
DENISE: You don't like it?
DAN: No, no, I do. I just noticed it has a Polo label. . . . I guess that brand costs a few dollars more.
DENISE: We don't always have to buy cheap. Besides, I got it on sale.
DAN: I was only commenting because we're strapped for money.
DENISE: I happen to like it, and I don't need to be Ms. Poverty all the time.
DAN: Can't I even say what I'm thinking without you going ballistic?

As the waiter serves their selections, they both feel the chill envelop their meal.

The Road to Power Snuggling

To some people, saving a few dollars on clothes versus buying a brand name might seem like a trivial issue, yet Dan and Denise grew irate as each defended their values. Denise prides herself on her choice of clothes. She enjoys receiving compliments on her good taste. But she is very sensitive to Dan's comments since she knows they are on a tight budget. At the same time, Dan is proud of his well-dressed wife, yet he prides himself on keeping a balanced budget. During their conversation, Denise magnifies the importance of her ability to dress fashionably, while Dan magnifies the importance of his ability to save money. Just as a magnifying glass exaggerates images, Dan and Denise's thoughts are irrationally amplified.

Using the magnifying glass, the issue is no longer about the Polo label or spending a few dollars more for a blouse. The issue expands as Denise reacts emotionally to Dan's comments. She sees this as a personal affront and believes Dan has no faith that she can manage money. She thinks, "I know how to buy quality clothes. If it were up to Dan, I'd be wearing rags. Next he'll tell me I overdo it when I buy groceries." Dan gets uptight because he feels that he needs to keep tabs on their finances, and he worries that he is losing control. He says to himself, "Our budget is tight enough. What if she continues spending wildly? We may not be able to replace the broken dishwasher." During their heated conversation, each feels they need to push for their own values. As we have discussed in previous sections, these values were developed in childhood, and they usually do not change.

Sustaining Your Snuggle

Together, think of disagreements that were magnified out of proportion. Looking back, replay one of your discussions and recognize the emotions that arose, overriding a more peaceful outcome. Begin using a calmer approach that is nonthreatening: take a deep breath; listen to each other's point of view; focus on your partner's feelings, even if you don't agree. When you understand the other's perspective, it becomes easier to reach a win-win resolution.

You Have to Get Rid of Your Stuff!

MEGAN: Chad, I can't take this anymore. Get rid of your stuff or I'll get rid of you! You've junked up the house with boxes of stuff you've never used, books you'll never read, tools you'll never need, a bread machine that's never kneaded bread, and smelly spray cans that will never, ever be sprayed.

CHAD: Hold on. When I need a tool, I'm not about to re-buy it. And what about you with your stuff?

MEGAN: What do you mean? What about me and my stuff?

CHAD: You save tons of ancient birthday cards that clutter drawers and—

MEGAN: Cards don't clutter. They hardly take up any space. Your stuff is big. So you want me to throw out the lovely cards that bring back memories?

CHAD: Look, just keep last year's cards. You know I have to keep my tools. I never know when I might need one.

MEGAN: But this house is a holy wreck. I can't live like this. Please, please toss some things out.

CHAD: My stuff isn't hurting you.

MEGAN, *stomping away:* Ugh!

The Road to Power Snuggling

E. B. White joked, "A home is like a reservoir equipped with a check valve: the valve permits influx but prevents outflow" ("Goodbye to Forty-Eighth Street," *Essays of E. B. White* [Harper & Row, New York, 1977]). Most families include the savers, sometimes certified pack rats, and the tossers, sometimes certified minimalists who feel the clothes on their back are all they will ever need. Relationships falter when the disparity between savers and tossers grates on each other's nerves and neither will bend.

There is common ground. Even pack rats can be convinced that some items will never be needed. And minimalists can be persuaded that some items used infrequently should be kept. We each have a right to be in charge of our stuff. At the same time, when space is tight, we should avoid using communal living areas to house our belongings. Instead, we need to look for out-of-the-way storage spots that will not inconvenience our partner.

Sustaining Your Snuggle

Does your partner collect an abundance of stuff? Or do they insist on keeping the house clutter-free? Work together to throw out unneeded items. Sell them, give them away, or donate them to charity.

Discuss the importance of saving some items that are of sentimental value as well as objects, such as tools, that may be needed in the future. A cooperative effort makes room for a more peaceful, loving relationship and clearer minds.

Why Do I Have to Do It All?

Sue made a list before she confronted Terry.

SUE: I have to make the kids' lunches and go to work. I do most of the cooking, supervise the kids' homework, schedule all our social events, and keep the calendar. Who calls the babysitters? When the plumbing backs up, who calls the plumber and stays home? It's just not fair.

TERRY: Look, you do a lot, but you don't do it all. Who washes the dishes after meals? Who keeps our expense account and tries to invest what little is left? Who takes care of the car? And I dropped the kids off at soccer just last week.

SUE: For the first time in months.

TERRY: I'm busy too. Don't I work more hours than you? You don't do it all.

The Road to Power Snuggling

We have found, more often than not, that one person—and frequently both partners—complain that they do it all. Sometimes a workload needs to be rebalanced. However, a strong partnership is not based on keeping tabs and equalizing chore time. Rather, it is built on cooperation and mutual support.

Sue may do too much because she does not feel that Terry can measure up to her standards. This provides Terry with an easy out. "After all," he may think, "why bother when what I do is *never* good enough?" A long-term relationship allows ample opportunities for us to use our talents as we adjust to life's changes. Long-term love means that when push comes to shove, we can and will unite to overcome our short-term stresses. When needed, Terry can step in and do the job. Sue can appreciate and accept his effort, which might be just adequate or even superior to her method.

On a daily basis, there is more harmony when we each contribute whatever is needed. The reward is a deeper feeling of connection and partners who appreciate each other's efforts. However, if either of us is agitated over what we feel is an unfair situation, action needs to be taken.

Sustaining Your Snuggle

Chances are, in the early part of your relationship, you were both conscientious about household responsibilities, and you went out of your way to please each other. Have you been able to sustain that level of collaboration? If you are overly burdened and resentful, it is time to review your schedules. Instead of pointing a finger, let your partner know of your concerns with "I" messages: "I feel like I'm handling way too much these days. My anxieties will calm down if I get more cooperation." Again using "I" messages, you can be more specific about your needs.

It may take several conversations to develop an agreeable plan. Validate that you are there for each other, and you will continue to be. Periodically, review the mix and make necessary adjustments.

When Your Partner Tries to Control You

JUAN: Pam, that's not a good toothpaste. Here, use mine. It's better.
PAM: Why? There's nothing wrong with mine.
JUAN: Well, mine is a new brand that I picked up, and I love it. Better protection against cavities, and see how shiny my teeth look?
PAM: Juan, I've been using my toothpaste forever. I'm happy with it, and I'm not interested in changing to your brand.

An hour later Juan and Pam are riding bikes in the park.

JUAN: Just coast now and enjoy it. Pretty soon, we'll have some tough hills with lots of pedaling.
PAM: Juan, would you please lay off! We've been on this trail a million times. Let me do my own thing.
JUAN: I don't get why you're so angry. I was only making a friendly suggestion.

The Road to Power Snuggling

In many relationships, one partner regularly tells the other what to do, what to eat, what is good or bad for them, and even what clothes to wear. These constant directives might persist for years, having negative impacts on both their relationship and their partner. If one is bombarded by commands, resentment replaces mutual respect. In contrast, a strong love relationship is based on respect and appreciation of each other's abilities to make decisions. A healthy relationship allows both partners to contribute ideas and preferences. Juan needs to recognize the dynamic he is creating, and he and Pam need to come together with opinions and facts, working toward a common goal.

The choices we make when we are part of a couple do not only affect us as individuals. They affect our partner and the relationship as a whole. The guidelines in the following paragraphs define the three types of decisions we make when we are in a relationship.

First are the decisions that we must make together. These include major decisions such as where to live, what kind of housing to rent or purchase, and how many children we want. Less important decisions that must be made together are where to vacation, what movies to see, and which friends to visit together.

We also make decisions individually that have a major impact on our partner. These decisions require that we consult each other. They include where we work and what kind of job we choose as well as purchases that affect our budget. Daily activities that affect the other person also fall under this category.

Finally we must make individual decisions separate from our partner. For these, we might wish to consult our partner, who could have a few suggestions. But the final decision should be our call. If our partner's suggestions feel like nagging, we should let them know.

Certainly Pam's choice of toothpaste and whether to coast her bike or pedal fit this category, and she reacted appropriately. Other individual decisions include which doctors to use, our choice of personal friends, what clothes to wear, hairstyles, and which hobbies we choose to pursue.

Sustaining Your Snuggle

If you feel like you are losing power when bombarded with advice or if your partner jumps in to make most of the decisions, it is time for a change. Discuss how you can use your different temperaments and strengths to support one another. Acknowledge that you each need to feel important. Always look for that delicate balance of being helpful rather than controlling. Since old habits are difficult to alter, periodically revisit this topic, promoting more equality in your relationship.

V

Is My Partner Crazy?

There are times when our ideas and our partner's ideas are so far apart that we feel the other one must be "off their rocker." As we examine our differences, we realize that there are ways to unravel the confusion and meet at a comfortable place somewhere in the middle.

Are You and Your Partner Living in the Same Country?

ROY: The brakes are wearing down on the Honda, and the oil needs to be changed.

JOAN: Yeah, I heard a squeak while I was driving with Martha to the PTA meeting. They had quite a crowd. I sure wish you could have come to the meeting and that you didn't have to stay home with the kids last night.

ROY: Maybe I can get Bob to drive to the game, and I'll drop the car off on the way.

JOAN: The teachers have too many students in the classroom. There's no way they can teach when the kids are all jumping around. They can't control them. The problem is getting worse, and we have to do something about it.

ROY: I better call now to see if I can take the car in early tomorrow morning. Then I should have it in time. It's supposed to be a great game. Joan, did you know they're tied for first place?

JOAN: I'm so upset about the class size. It's terrible. I hope you'll write to the school board. We need a forceful letter.

ROY: What?

This couple cannot hear each other if one is in "Joan-land" speaking "Joanish" and the other is in "Roy-land" speaking "Royish." As long as they each remain in their own separate countries, they will continue to be disconnected mentally and emotionally. They're speaking different languages and are unable to cross the border and join their partner if they aren't willing to learn the other's lingo.

The Road to Power Snuggling

We each have our own interests, and we are passionate about them. However, to continue our friendship and our romance, we need to regularly stop and take notice of where our partner is living and what language they are speaking. To reconnect, we must walk over the bridge into their country. By listening attentively to our partner's words, focusing on their body language, and relating to their culture, our relationship will flourish. The goal is to pick up and connect where the other leaves off.

If Roy and Joan paid more attention to the words and priorities of the other, their conversation might sound more like this:

ROY: The brakes are wearing down on the Honda, and the oil needs to be changed.
JOAN, *watching Roy purse his lips with a worried look:* Right, that can be dangerous. I heard a squeak when I drove Martha to the PTA meeting. Will you be able to take the car to the garage?
ROY: I thought I'd drop it off before Bob and I go to the game. How was the PTA meeting?
JOAN: Oh, great attendance! I wish you could've been there. We decided to write to the school board about the teacher problem. The overcrowded classrooms are terrible.
ROY: Good idea to write to the school board. (*Roy pats Joan's shoulder.*) We've got to get smaller class sizes. Bob and I can try to think of some ideas for the letter while we drive to the game.
JOAN: Thanks. We'd love your input. By the way, I read that our pitchers are terrific this season, especially Findley, who's starting. It should be a great game.

Sustaining Your Snuggle

Think of conversations you have had when you felt you were disconnected from each other. As you hear your partner talk, take in their body language as well as their words. This will allow you to pick up on their emotions. Ask questions to learn more and show you care. If your partner says something that you do not understand, ask more questions.

There will be times when you are busy and are not available to listen. You might have to say, "Sorry, I can't focus on that right now, but I'd love to hear what you have to say later." Then offer a time when it will be convenient for both of you.

Try visiting each other's country frequently during the week. Congratulate yourself every time you cross that bridge.

Analytical Amanda

You might have spotted Amanda in the grocery store with her eyes focused on the calculator of her smartphone. Or you may have seen her at the PTA meeting when she asked how many school days and snow days were scheduled this year compared to last. When Amanda makes suggestions for a restaurant, she describes in detail the size of their portions, the price of each entree, the distance from home, and the likelihood of getting a good table at different times.

One day her husband, Alan, could no longer keep silent:

ALAN: Amanda, I really want to go to Flannery's for dinner.
AMANDA: Flannery's? But Alan, you know their portions are small, and the prices are high. Besides, it takes 27 minutes to drive there without traffic and 45 minutes in rush hour. Why go there?
ALAN: Because I like eating there.
AMANDA: But . . .
ALAN: I want to go there tonight.
AMANDA: Okay. This time.

As they sat in Flannery's, Alan glowed. Amanda said, "You really seem to like it here. Why?" Alan's words flowed. He mentioned the delicious corned beef and cabbage with soda bread, the warmth of the servers, the music, and the beautiful flowers behind the glass doors. He said Flannery's reminded him of being a child in Dublin.

As he spoke, Amanda began to understand that feelings could trump prices and portions and driving distances. She thought of the good times she and Alan had when they first met. She realized that somehow they accepted each other's wishes, they went wherever they wanted without planning, and they thoroughly enjoyed themselves.

The Road to Power Snuggling

We were initially attracted to our partner because of our different temperaments. At first, Alan liked the idea that Amanda was quick with figures and details. That was never his forte, and he found it intriguing. He still likes the idea that he can depend on her for schedules and details. However, in this situation, he was looking forward to a quiet, intimate dinner in one of his favorite settings. And he had zero interest in Amanda's logic.

At first, Amanda was attracted to Alan because he was laid-back and an agreeable kind of guy. She still appreciates that quality in him, but she realizes that he is now more likely to take a stand. She is learning to appreciate his opinions, which can benefit them both.

Too often couples argue over facts to make their case, when the real challenge has more to do with being together and enjoying the moment, wherever that might be. For love, there is no measurement of quantity or quality. We just know that it feels good, and we like being there.

Sustaining Your Snuggle

Is one of you more into details, while the other one opts for the emotional benefits of just being in the moment? How does your partner feel if you try to override their desires with facts and figures? Do they take a position and try to convince you otherwise? Do they let it go and become resentful?

In many situations, you should set aside your facts. Instead, reach out with understanding. Save the details for circumstances that require additional information. Take a risk, and let yourself enjoy your partner's choice. View the "beautiful flowers behind the glass doors."

Ms. Dreamer vs. Ms. Practical

Kim and Alex were searching the Internet for a winter vacation spot. They thought they agreed about their destination until their conflicting priorities came to light.

KIM: At least we know we want to escape to a warm place with pretty landscapes and sunsets. Oh, and a sandy beach we can see from the balcony.

ALEX: Well, that depends on the price. Sunsets and landscapes are great, but if it's cheaper a block from the beach, that would be better. And I need an Internet connection.

KIM: You know, I really need to see the water. We can stay a shorter time if it's too expensive.

ALEX: I thought we agreed it would be exactly two weeks. Once we fly that far, it doesn't pay to cut down on the days. If we divide the total cost by the number of days, the per-day cost can't be over our budget.

KIM: With a pretty view and good music nearby, it'll be worth it. I just need a warm place to unwind, walk out to the beach, and read under an umbrella.

ALEX: That's fine. But the room has to be fairly large and have a shower, not a bathtub.

KIM: For a couple of weeks, the room size doesn't matter. We'll be outside most of the time anyway.

The Road to Power Snuggling

With many couples, partners fall into one of two types: the dreamer—creative, unscheduled, with a focus on fun and what feels good—and the practical one—a planner and scheduler who quantifies the costs and benefits and calculates the pros and cons. When buying a house, the dreamer takes one look and thinks, "This feels good. It's beautiful. Let's buy it." The practical one walks in and thinks, "Let's measure the room sizes, check the heat and air controls, and request copies of utility bills."

Both dreamer and practical personalities are needed, whether we are planning a vacation, buying a house, or simply shopping in a store, but disputes occur when either partner overemphasizes one quality over the other. The philosophy of "Life is to have fun" does not always reconcile with the more matter-of-fact approach, "We have to check every detail." To overcome those basic disagreements, we need to understand our differences, appreciate them, and use them to our advantage. Accepting and using the value of both the pleasurable and the practical personalities opens new doors in our relationship as we express differing opinions.

Sustaining Your Snuggle

Examine a disagreement that resulted from the differences between the dreamer and practical personality types. Knowing your partner as you do, does their position make sense? Without giving up your preferences, validate what your partner is saying: "It makes sense that you would want to walk right out onto the beach. I know how much you love the ocean," or "I get what you're saying. I know you worry about the extra cost closer to the beach. You're trying to save us money." Validating can work wonders since your partner will be more likely to compromise when they know you understand them.

Neat vs. Messy

The Odd Couple, a 1968 film written by Neil Simon, was later adapted into the television series that starred Tony Randall as Felix Unger, the neatnik, and Jack Klugman as Oscar Madison, the messy one. Felix and Oscar are two divorced men sharing a New York City apartment. They routinely squabble over the issues that arise as a result of Felix's compulsive organization and neatness conflicting with Oscar's extreme disorganization.

Felix's obsessive personality is illustrated in the following memorable scene from the original film. Oscar complains, "I can't take it anymore, Felix, I'm cracking up. Everything you do irritates me. And when you're not here, the things I know you're gonna do when you come in irritate me. You leave me little notes on my pillow. Told you 158 times I can't stand little notes on my pillow. 'We're all out of cornflakes. F.U.' Took me three hours to figure out F.U. was Felix Unger!"

Neat versus messy can escalate to become the major issue with some couples:

SONIA: Why do you say I'm a neat freak? I'm just average. Besides, neatness is next to godliness.

JOHN: The saying is "Cleanliness is next to godliness."

SONIA: Same thing.

JOHN: You're saying it's normal to fold underwear before putting it away, to line up every kitchen chair after each meal, to fluff each pillow every time I get up from the sofa, to alphabetize our books on the bookcase, and to make the bed just seconds after we get up.

SONIA: At least I don't leave crumbs on the table to feed the bugs and spread my papers all over the place. And when you do make the bed, it's lopsided. You never know where you put your wallet, and every night you drop your clothes on the floor.

JOHN: But they're in a nice, neat pile.

SONIA: I can't stand it!

JOHN: I hate this! I can't feel comfortable in my own home.

The Road to Power Snuggling

Some people like all of their magazines and DVDs organized so they can grab them with their eyes closed. Others want to keep their belongings where they left them for easy access. Some look forward to a major house cleaning each year. Others fear discarding anything. The topic of neatness versus messiness is a common complaint of couples. When we move in together we bring our household habits with us. From the time we are young we have established a method of organization or disorganization that works for us. So it is not surprising that what we think is a reasonable way of living appears to be extreme or too laid-back for our partner.

In *A Perfect Mess: The Hidden Benefits of Disorder*, by Eric Abrahamson and David H. Freedman, the authors argue that messy people are more productive because orderliness takes more time and quashes creativity. In contrast, neat people argue that because they are more organized, they save time by knowing where to find things. Understandably, these different approaches often cause friction in our relationship. It is difficult for a "messy" person to wrap their mind around someone who insists on keeping everything in order. Ironically, the untidy people need tidy partners to help keep order. And the organized people need less orderly partners who tend to be more laid-back and accepting of their environment and their situation. With the use of both styles, we can find a balance that feels more comfortable for each of us, helping to maintain a calmer environment.

Sustaining Your Snuggle

There are limits to what each of you can tolerate, and compromise is needed. Accepting each other's wishes and working toward a balance will diminish arguments. You will never convince your partner that your way is the right way, but you can agree to tone down the extremes.

Listen fully to each other about the advantages of different organizational methods. Take time to list the most bothersome behaviors associated with each other's neat versus messy ways. Then find ways to accommodate both of your needs, creating a more positive environment for the entire household. For the good of your relationship, create some movement toward the middle of the road.

You're Always Late!

MATTHEW: Come on, Tracy, we're gonna miss our plane.
TRACY: Matthew, lighten up. I just need another minute. There's little traffic on Sunday. As usual, we'll end up waiting for our plane for over an hour.
MATTHEW: What if there's a freeway accident? You know how long it takes to go through security. It'll be a bummer if we miss our plane.
TRACY: Just a few more minutes. I just have to—
MATTHEW: You can finish that in the car.

Sound familiar? Matthew is becoming more anxious by the minute. At the same time, Tracy is nervous because Mathew is pressuring her. He wants to get to the airport two hours in advance. She's happy to get there just in time to slip onto the plane.

The Road to Power Snuggling

We all have to pay attention to time and are born with an internal clock telling us what it means to be on time. Nevertheless, people differ in their feelings about time schedules, and many of us somehow select a partner who adheres to a clock different from our own. We may need to meet the same time schedule when we travel together, see movies together, and attend events together, but time conflicts can go on for years unless we figure out how to adjust to each other.

Recognition of their differing scheduling needs can help Matthew and Tracy reconcile their divergent time clocks. Matthew needs to get to the airport well in advance so he can take his time and relax before boarding. Tracy needs to realize that just thinking about missing the plane creates a high level of stress in Matthew. She can help him by getting to the airport early and hassle-free. Then, without resentment, she can read, use her cell phone, or find other activities while they wait at the airport. This becomes a win-win situation since Matthew will be calmer, and Tracy will not feel pressured by his anxiety. When it comes to an event such as a party, where being late will not have major consequences, Matthew needs to accept

Tracy's more relaxed clock. While Tracy is getting ready, he can read or watch TV and refrain from nagging.

Sustaining Your Snuggle

Review instances when you disagreed on time issues. Each of you should define what important deadlines mean. When you have plans as a couple, agree to coordinate the details. However, calculating the minutes needed to get to a plane or a party should not be your main concern. Instead, think of ways to relieve each other's anxiety. If help is needed, pitch in without resentment. It pays off.

Eric Efficiency

You might know Eric. At work they call him "Eric Efficiency." He can tell you how to best organize any project and the fastest way to complete it at the lowest cost. He never loses his cool, and he is on task and relaxed throughout the day. His supervisor thinks he's the greatest, and his coworkers love him.

One evening, Eric walks into his house and his wife, Heidi, greets him with a hug and a kiss, but he can see she is in a tizzy.

ERIC: What's the matter?
HEIDI: You cannot believe my day! The traffic going to work was terrible *and* Ellie skinned her knee at school, so I had to pick her up in the middle of the day *and* our housekeeper canceled *and* the groceries melted in the back seat of the car *and* the dog was sick to his stomach *and* . . .

Eric Efficiency quickly sums up the situation. He grabs a pad and a pen and lists each event. Then he begins to tell Heidi exactly how she could have avoided some of the problems. This, he explains, will allow her to prepare for next time. He even offers to show her how she could vacuum the house quickly, without the housekeeper.

At this point, Heidi erupts, screaming. It sets the scene for a movie that would have made Steven Spielberg proud. Eric stands frozen and puzzled. Why would Heidi reject his efficiency skills? They love his skills at the office.

Eric loses his cool, yells back, and slams the door. He then drives to the office to finish some work. When he is able to catch his breath and relax in the sanctuary of his office, he wonders why Heidi was so angry. After all, he tried to help her in the most efficient way.

The Road to Power Snuggling

Fortunately, over time Eric learned that the skills required to operate a successful business are very different from those needed to create and maintain a loving relationship. The chart below highlights these differences.

Business Skills	Love Skills
Focus on facts and solutions.	Focus on empathy and emotions.
Organization and planning are critical.	Caring and consideration are critical.
Keep your emotions under control.	Be emotionally open, without overburdening your partner.
Trust, but be cautious of customers and coworkers.	Acceptance and trust are essential.
Respect competence and quickly correct incompetence.	Respect your partner for their character, even when they make mistakes.
Be committed to your company but look for better opportunities.	Be committed to long-term love, realizing you will have ups and downs.
Intimacy in the office is unacceptable.	Intimacy with your partner is very important.

Months later, having analyzed which behaviors and mindsets are more suited to the office, Eric arrives home and finds Heidi in a tizzy. He listens carefully to her problems and gives her a hug. He says, "It must have been a terrible day. Anyone would be upset after a day like that." He listens and listens and then lets her rest. He offers no advice and no solutions. Later, with Eric's support, Heidi calms down and comes to terms with the dilemmas of her day.

Sustaining Your Snuggle

When you have had a bad day, how do you each react? Are you respectful of your partner's needs when they feel distressed? Read their body language to determine what they want from you. Start with a hug. It shows you care. They may need time alone to calm down or they may need a sympathetic ear to listen without offering suggestions.

When you have had a bad day, what do you need most from your partner? If you do not share your thoughts, your partner can only guess what you want. Talk about behaviors that would be helpful to each of you.

What Could She Be Thinking?

REBECCA: Why would anyone want to play bridge for a whole weekend? It's such a waste of time.
TONY: And you think seeing those tear-jerker movies with your friends and reading celebrity magazines is time well spent?
REBECCA: Well, understanding human emotions is worthwhile. It deals with life.
TONY: And trying to outthink a bridge team prepares you to deal with life's struggles. It's much more useful than watching those emotional flicks.

The Road to Power Snuggling

Tony and Rebecca have no interest in each other's hobbies, and they find it difficult to appreciate the other's activity preferences or why they find their activities gratifying. They are unable to place themselves in the other's position and understand the way the other thinks and feels. The following experiment demonstrates the importance of understanding what the other person is thinking and feeling.

The Sally-Anne Test is a classic experiment that evaluates the social skills and thinking of young children. It was developed by Simon Baron-Cohen of Cambridge University. This simple yet highly predictive test works like this: A young child watches an adult, Sally, place a marble in a basket and leave the room. While she is gone, the child watches another adult, Anne, remove the marble from the basket and put it into a closet. Before Sally returns to the room, the child is asked, "Where will Sally look for the marble?" Children pass the test if they indicate that Sally will look for the marble in the basket where she last saw the marble. However, almost all children under the age of four say Sally will look in the closet, where the marble is now hidden. They believe that what they see, everyone sees. A year later, they would understand that Sally does not have the same information they do, and they would expect Sally to look in the basket where she had originally placed the marble.

As adults, we easily pass this test. However, like Rebecca and Tony, we frequently fail a similar test. We tend to think that what we believe, others should believe and what we feel, others should feel. Instead of focusing on what is in our partner's mind, we try to project our feelings and values onto them. Our beliefs tend to be so powerful that we think others who disagree must have poor judgment, are lacking facts, or may even be lying to us about how they feel. As a result of such thinking, Rebecca and Tony are unable to find each other's "marble."

Partners who have lost sight of each other's distinct perspectives may say, "You shouldn't worry about getting to the lecture late. We've got plenty of time;" "You can't be hungry again. You just ate;" or "Of course the beach would be a better vacation than touring a hot city. That's a no-brainer!" There is nothing wrong with stating our feelings as long as we open the door for our partner to express theirs as well. Instead of assuming our partner agrees with us, we could say, "I like vacationing at the beach. What do you think?" Sometimes, we are like the young child who cannot enter into Sally's mind. However, unlike the three year old, our brain has developed and we are capable of knowing what our partner is thinking and feeling.

Sustaining Your Snuggle

It takes emotional strength to find your partner's marble. Uncover it by asking and listening. Then ask and listen again. Temporarily let go of where you see the marble and embrace your partner's thoughts, as an actor embraces the thoughts of a character. You may think you are giving up your viewpoint by encouraging your partner to express their perspective, but listening to their point of view does not mean agreeing. It just means understanding. Take turns fully presenting each side of an issue without interruption. As you listen to your partner, keep track of where that marble can be found.

Understanding Angry Andy

ANDY: Linda! I just asked you to pick up some bagels while you were at the store. I didn't ask you to reconstruct the universe!

For years, Linda listened to Andy's anger. He was angry at home and angry at work. Andy would embarrass her by arguing with their friends over everything from politics to baseball scores. She constantly told him it was fine to disagree, but his shrill voice and put-downs were inexcusable. Now she heard her own anger erupt:

LINDA: Andy, that's enough! I'm tired of shopping for you and catering to you and seeing our kids collapse under your anger and making excuses for you when friends complain. I'm done with this.

She bolted from the house, slammed the door, disappeared into the car, and drove off to Sandy's house to unwind.

That night, Linda dreamed that she walked past Andy's computer room and into another room. She leaned against the wall, and a door opened next to a circular staircase. After many upward turns, she found herself in an attic. In the far corner stood a huge glass jug with Andy's name on it. A bright red sign floated near the top of the jug. It read, "Anger." Three blue signs floated lower down: "Hurt," "Sad," and "Lonely." Resting at the bottom of the jug were two green signs labeled "Compassion" and "Love."

In her dream, Linda took a stick and stirred the contents gently. Some of the Anger at the top slowly dissipated. Then the other signs floated toward the top, all in a row. She bubbled with enthusiasm when she turned and met Andy at the staircase.

ANDY: So you found my secret jug.
LINDA: Uh-huh. I forgot you had all those wonderful parts.
ANDY: Well, I couldn't let people see them. That's too dangerous.
LINDA: I guess so, but I'm glad I found them. Maybe I can help you use all of those hidden parts and still feel safe.

ANDY: Even anger?

LINDA: Even anger, when necessary, if it's expressed without hurting others. As long as you also bring the other good parts down from the attic. Eventually, I think revealing your hurt, sad, and lonely parts will free you to use more of the compassion and love you have hidden. I know you have these qualities because you used them many times when we first met. I bet we'll be much happier if we both make more use of these parts.

ANDY: Thanks for stirring my emotions. Maybe now I'll feel free to express all my parts.

Linda awoke and felt encouraged. Her dream paved the way toward helping Andy recover the love and compassion that were buried within him.

The Road to Power Snuggling

Mark Twain noted, "Anger is an acid that can do more harm to the vessel in which it is stored than to anything on which it is poured." Continually holding anger inside is physically and mentally damaging. It can raise our blood pressure, cause ulcers, migraines, depression, and a host of other illnesses. A fulfilling life requires that we express our anger, hurt, sadness, and loneliness so kindness and love can emerge. However, we must express these emotions, without blame, so that our partner can hear us.

We can help our partner and ourselves by understanding that below the anger lies a whole spectrum of emotions that developed over a lifetime of experiences. Understanding the roots of theses emotions makes it easier to listen to our partner with compassion.

Sustaining Your Snuggle

Expressing anger is acceptable if it is not used to hurt your partner. We all become angry over traffic, office conflicts, or daily annoyances. We also become angry over our partner's behavior. In these situations, speak with them about your feelings. Omit such phrases as "You always" or "You never." Learn to say "I feel" instead.

Help your partner remove that protective barrier of anger and stubbornness by listening with compassion. They can then more easily tap into and enjoy their loving and caring parts.

Heather the Helper

Heather was unhappy and harried. For years she had been helping her children, helping her neighbors and friends, helping her coworkers, and of course helping her husband, Harry. She took pride when friends referred to her as "Supermom." You may have seen her drop her boys off at soccer, race to the grocery store, and return home just in time to meet the plumber. Her computer calendar was packed. She made sure to cook healthy foods, clean meticulously, and teach the boys to write thank-you notes. She didn't dare ask Harry to do much because he would always "screw up."

She confided to her neighbor:

HEATHER: I'm so frustrated. This isn't the life I envisioned. I have way too much to do, and I'm the only one who can do it. Harry will never change.
PAULA: Harry can help. He can cook some dinners and drive the kids to soccer practice.
HEATHER: Harry? He couldn't make tea with a tea bag if I boiled the water, and the last time he drove the kids to soccer, he was twenty minutes late.
PAULA: Well, Pete couldn't cook either when we first got married, but now he bakes five-layer cakes.
HEATHER: Harry's different. He can't do anything right. I'm afraid I'll be frustrated forever. Harry and the boys totally depend on me.

On a wintry morning, Heather walked outside. She thought it was water, but a sheet of ice lay near her car. She slipped and became airborne. A leg and an arm slammed against the ice and both were broken. After the first shooting pain, she knew that Harry would have to take over while she was laid up.

From her hospital bed, Heather told Harry to check the schedule. She was specific about how to handle the household chores. When she finally arrived home, she found Harry hadn't checked the schedule, and he had barely followed her orders. But somehow, he and the boys had survived.

They bought carryout only once. Harry dug out a cookbook and baked lasagna from scratch, served with a salad and garlic bread. He bought plantains, which he thought were bananas, and learned to fry them. The boys helped cook and even added veggies. They were late to soccer only once. Harry was upbeat. Heather noticed a spot of spaghetti sauce on the rug but made no comment. She found a broken plate and disposed of it quietly.

The Road to Power Snuggling

Heather began to understand that family peace and pride were much more important than her "right" way. She realized Harry's new talents were really old, hidden talents that finally had been allowed to surface. She saw how her frequent kvetching had paralyzed him. As Heather softened, Harry felt appreciated. She had to compromise some of her values, but she was much less stressed. As Heather became more accepting, Harry worked harder to please her. They gradually became Helpful Harry and Happy Heather.

Sustaining Your Snuggle

Do either of you find it difficult to delegate jobs and accept the outcome if it is not exactly to your liking? It is time to entrust some of your responsibilities to your partner and reduce the household stress level. You need not be incapacitated to change family dynamics. You only have to compromise some of your ways.

Accept the help your partner provides and show gratitude, even when they take on a task differently. You might find new approaches appealing. As you enable your partner to help, use those moments of freedom it creates to appreciate their gift of time through meditation or rest. Find ways for your children to pitch in, starting when they can walk. Then relax and dispose of broken plates quietly.

VI

In-Laws, Outlaws, and Other Complex Forces

Before we met our love partner, we developed individual values and habits. We shared our lives with family and friends. Consequently, learning to accept and adapt to another person's beliefs and practices—not to mention accommodating in-laws—requires a great deal of understanding, empathy, and compromise.

You Love Your Mom More Than Me

DAWN: Your mom's calling again. (*Dawn frowns, hands the phone to David, and walks away.*)
DAVID: Yeah, Mom. Uh-huh . . . When do you need it done? I can't Monday, but how 'bout Tuesday? Yeah, I told you that when you called a few hours ago. I've got to go; Dawn's waiting. Bye.
DAWN: When are you going to cater to me like you cater to her? We're the ones who are married. There's no way I can feel close to her when she calls all the time. When will we ever have a private life together?
DAVID: Well, she did give birth to me, and she raised me. The least I can do is talk to her when she calls. She's lonely. Since Dad died, I need to be available.
DAWN: You not only talk to her, but you go to her house regularly. You know, she's not helpless. She has a separate life, or at least I would love to think so.

The Road to Power Snuggling

Dawn and David have been married for years. Throughout that time, it seems that David has been constantly on the phone with his mother. Dawn tries to ignore it, but at times she can't help blowing up. Some of us juggle this well, but for many, daily tensions rise and the emotional bond between partners weakens. Of course, the situation could be reversed, with Dawn spending too much time on the phone with Mom, children, relatives, or friends. Jealousies often occur in families. If one person feels their partner is spending too much time or giving too much attention to another—whether it be Mom, Dad, or friends—it is time to discuss the matter. We need to set boundaries with others so they do not interrupt our valuable couple's time.

In the example above, David and Dawn need to acknowledge what is happening and how it is impacting their family. The solution lies in balancing everyone's needs. David needs to set limits on calls and visits and inform everyone, especially Mom. He should let Mom know which times are convenient for him and Dawn and which times are inconvenient. If necessary, he can allow voicemail to take over and delay responding to emails.

Sustaining Your Snuggle

As a couple, your primary relationship is with your partner. Of course, this does not mean you should ignore others, especially relatives and good friends. Maintaining a balance can be a juggling act since all close relationships require time and effort. Who are the people important to you, other than your partner? Is time and effort spent with them infringing on your relationship? Does your partner give hints of annoyance and frustration? Be sensitive to their needs early on. When you notice signs of resentment, develop a plan to provide an appropriate balance.

Meddling Mom

ERICA: Mom's coming over. She says she wants to take a photo of our sofa so she can match the curtains.

GREGORY: Enough already. She matches anything with everything. I'm afraid if I stay in the living room too long, I'll also be matched up. Besides, when she matches, it costs us a bundle. Maybe I like mismatched.

ERICA: Well, you have to give her credit. She's an interior decorator, and she knows what looks good. And she gets discounts on almost everything.

GREGORY: Look, Erica, things are going too far. I thought she'd make an occasional suggestion, with us having the final say. Now she says, "You really should have these chairs and paint your bedroom this color." I'm over it.

ERICA: We did finally compromise on the color more to your liking, but the other stuff she suggested makes sense.

GREGORY: Erica, it's not just decorating. She's into *everything*. She claims she's merely suggesting, but she tells us what foods to eat, what appliances to buy, and where to shop for clothes. Oh, yesterday she said I'd look better with a buzz cut! I need your help. We have to let her know that she can't be so intrusive.

ERICA: Gregory, we can't ignore her. She's my mother. Your dad regularly gives you advice.

GREGORY: Yeah, but it's limited to financial stuff, and he doesn't bombard us with his ideas. I wouldn't mind an occasional suggestion. But daily? It's ridiculous. We're a couple. We have to live our own lives.

Erica's mother may be a wonderful interior decorator and a loving, caring woman. However, she's interfering with Gregory and Erica's life, to the point where they are continually battling each other over her controlling ways. Whether it is a meddling mother, father, Aunt Matilda, or a best friend, if either partner feels overwhelmed when an outsider tries to manage their life, it is time to set boundaries.

The Road to Power Snuggling

It is not uncommon for parents to feel unneeded when their child leaves them for their own partner. If we understand our parents' intention, we know they are only trying to stay linked to us and be helpful. How do we find a balance between their desire to remain close and our own need for independence and privacy as a couple?

When we decide to become a couple, we buy into the other's family. But we need not accept continuous intrusion. We can accommodate family and friends while staying firm in our commitment to each other. When others intrude, we need to discuss the situation and agree on ways to politely set limits. Building a firm line of defense will protect our relationship and balance our connection with others.

Showing a united front as a couple can also prevent problems when we are presented with parental "gifts" of money. Parents may offer financial help but with strings attached: "I'm giving you this money to be used only on a washer and dryer." Some parents give without expecting anything in return. Others give generously; however, if an argument develops between them and their children, the children might hear, "After all we've done for you, the least you can do is visit us more often," "Listen to our advice," or "You used our gift for that?" So beware of the strings.

Sustaining Your Snuggle

Find ways to balance your needs with your parents' needs. Zero in on your own feelings. Are you both okay with the amount of time spent with parents on the phone or in person? Do your parents respect your decisions?

Engineering an appropriate balance requires regular discussions as a couple and an understanding with your parents from the get-go of your relationship with your partner. At times, you probably enjoy the closeness of relatives and appreciate some advice, whether it involves advice on a recipe, training your dog, or supporting your children. Yet, when parents or others invade your turf, you must weigh their needs against your own. Be frank with a meddler. Let them know that their intrusions are harming your marriage. A loving relationship is too important to be jeopardized by a meddling mom.

Balancing a Blended Family

REBECCA: I know you've got issues with Shannon and that she keeps telling you her dad is nicer and more lenient. But it's hard at her age to adjust to two fathers.

WALTER: I hear you. But I don't get any respect from her. She obviously doesn't like me, and she has no problem showing it.

REBECCA: Well, don't think I can't see Jimmy rolling his eyes when I ask him to do something. That hurts a lot.

The Road to Power Snuggling

Rebecca and Walter's discussion relates to one of many challenges that face blended families. The traditional family, a first marriage with two parents and two children, is no longer the norm. Today, families come in every size and type. There are blended families, sometimes called stepfamilies, single-parent families, and gay and lesbian families. Children may be born to the first marriage, be products of the new relationship, or be adopted. If we add prior partners—the parent of our children or our current partner's children—we have a variety of people who somehow need to find ways of getting along.

About 65 percent of remarriages include children from prior marriages. Two people have issues of their own, but when families are merged, there are new complications. However, establishing a new family will work well if we follow certain guidelines. These include:

- Plan before you move in together. Talk about expectations and how you intend to parent. Once you agree, discuss your intentions with the children.
- Limit the changes children face when families are initially merged. If possible, continue with the same schools, time schedules, and traditions.
- Don't expect to immediately fall in love with your partner's children or for them to quickly accept you. Give it time, and connect by interacting.

- Encourage the children to express their feelings in this new environment, and listen without judgment.
- Insist on respect. This means children must respect both partners and each other. It also means parents must show consideration for all the children.
- Live life together. Take children to events as a group. Show them that you are working as a team to become a new family. Limit your expectations by allowing for flexibility and not insisting on perfection.

Somehow, most families survive all the confusion, and they do what everybody does: work, go to school, plan holiday parties, and live life fully.

With a blended family, it is especially important to adjust our behavior as circumstances change. Parents need not beat themselves up if they do not always come to happy solutions, like the Brady Bunch. That rarely happens. However, calm and thoughtful communication is key as we consider everyone's needs.

Sustaining Your Snuggle

To assure a smooth transition, it is essential to plan ahead before you move in together and establish a new family. Give your children ample opportunity to get to know your partner and their children before you move. Make sure that each member of the combined family understands what is occurring and has input into what is planned.

After you make tentative plans with your partner, consult each child so they feel a party to the decisions. Allow your children to fully express their feelings. Expect a variety of emotions to be voiced, from fear to great pleasure. Accept their emotions, whatever they may be. Let them know that you will adjust the household rules as situations require, and that you and your partner will be working together to ensure each child is treated fairly.

Think of this new adventure as positive. Chances are that over time the children will follow suit and be upbeat as well.

Easing Our Hectic Lives

It's morning. Troy and Tiffany are struggling to get out of the house.

TROY: Where are the umbrellas? We can't get the kids to school without them.
TIFFANY: Didn't you check the weather last night? I'm trying to make lunches.
TROY: My meeting is promptly at nine. I'll never make it on time.
TIFFANY: Well, with the traffic, I'll probably be late to the office too.
TROY: And Jason can't find his shoes. Where are they?
TIFFANY: Beats me. Did you check under his bed?

Somehow, Troy and Tiffany eventually manage to fall out of the house. This rushed, disorganized pattern has continued for years.

On the next block, Joe and April, who are about the same age, also with two children, enjoy a fairly relaxed morning. After completing all their tasks, April grabs the kids' ponchos from the hooks near the door, slips them onto the kids, and helps them into the car. She drops them off at school and takes her time driving to work.

The Road to Power Snuggling

In the previous scenario, both couples' marriages have had ups and downs, and both couples are attentive to their children's needs. Why then are Joe and April able to leave the house with much less commotion than Troy and Tiffany? The key is how Joe and April summon information found in the basal ganglia of their brains. The basal ganglia is a very small part of the brain, located deep inside our head above the brain stem, that allows us to systematically store a sequence of memories or actions for unconscious recall. In effect, this part of our brain operates as our "autopilot." In the 1990s, researchers studying both humans and mice discovered that series of actions, once learned, can be recalled as "chunks." While we are "chunking," we automatically carry out a series of tasks that are sometimes quite sophisticated, yet our brain uses very little energy in the process. Hence, our stress is minimal.

To reduce the anxiety behind our routines, we must begin chunking. When we awaken in the morning and glance at the clock, we have begun a chunk. A series of actions follow, such as washing up, getting dressed, and glancing out the window to check the weather. We have repeated these tasks hundreds of times, yet if questioned, we may not know which sock we slip on first or if we glanced at the mirror before brushing our teeth. It is not necessary to remember these details because they have been "copied and pasted" into our brain's basal ganglia. Our autopilot guides us, reducing stress, and freeing up time to concentrate on more pleasurable moments together.

Sustaining Your Snuggle

Think about deliberate actions you take. Then list actions you perform automatically. How can you structure your routines and schedules so that more actions become commonplace, allowing your autopilot to take over? Smooth the transition for both you and your partner by agreeing on regular time schedules and finding a special place for commonly used household objects. Encourage each other's chunking recall as much as possible by introducing minimal interruptions when the other is in the "zone."

Life changes require new or revised chunks. During a transitional period, stress increases but will later diminish as new chunks are substituted. Reduce tension by using the basal ganglia.

Help! I Need Time for Myself!

Nicole could barely breathe with everything that was going on. Brad had business in Dallas, and both kids were sick with the flu. Nicole didn't know yet whether she would have to miss work again. And of course this morning the toilet decided to overflow.

The phone rings, and Nicole's babysitter says she can't come because her brother-in-law is sick. Nicole starts to ask why the brother-in-law's illness has anything to do with it, but she stops short. "Will you be able to come on Thursday?" she asks. The sitter hesitates, "That depends." Nicole thinks, "I hate this! If only I could have a few hours to myself."

Later that night, after the kids are finally in bed, she collapses fully clothed on top of the quilt. Her dream is vivid. She is sitting on a tree branch next to a stream, surrounded by tall pine trees. Occasionally, fish splash at the water's surface. She's alone at last, reading a book. A robin begins to chirp, "Watcha reading? Watcha reading?" The robin tells Nicole how she flies away from her flock when there's too much commotion. Nicole feels cozy.

The Road to Power Snuggling

The author Pearl S. Buck said in a 1959 article in the *New York Post,* "Inside myself is a place where I live all alone, and that's where I renew my springs that never dry up." We all need some time and space for ourselves. We cannot function or enjoy life without a regular time to relax, to reflect, and to do what we want. For our mental health, we need to find private time for ourselves and for our partner, preferably daily. Using precious moments to regroup leaves us in a better frame of mind. When we listen to our soul, it is easier to listen to our partner.

Sustaining Your Snuggle

Do either of you ever feel like you are being smothered with too much of everything—job, kids, budgets, housework, and other commitments?

When you are at your wit's end, how do you cope? Are you both able to take the necessary private time you need? If not, talk about each of your requirements. Develop a plan and follow through. Offer your partner alone time freely, lovingly, and without resentment. The reward will be two relaxed people who become more available for each other.

You Know How Men Are!

Anna and Jack are having dinner with Gail and Doug. As Anna begins her joke, Jack starts to shake his head, knowing what she is up to.

ANNA: You know the difference between today's men and those in Biblical times? (*Silence*)
ANNA: No difference. The children of Israel wandered around the desert for forty years. Even in Biblical times men wouldn't ask for directions!
(*Both women laugh as the men shrug and look down.*)
DOUG: A man says to his friend, "I haven't spoken to my wife in eighteen months." The friend asks, "Why not?" The man says, "I don't like to interrupt her."
(*Both men chuckle.*)

As Anna and Doug illustrate, both men and women can show gender bias.

The Road to Power Snuggling

Most people are bothered when they hear humor that involves race, religion, sexual preferences, or disabilities. Yet we have all heard words, phrases, and jokes that demean, ignore, or stereotype members of either sex, needlessly calling attention to gender. Sexist jokes flood TV programs, the Internet, and public conversation. Over the years, we have known many men and women who are sensitive when they hear a joke about their gender, but they continue to tell jokes about the opposite sex.

Unfortunately, this type of humor provokes conflicts between the sexes. True, there are differences between the brains and the behaviors of men and women. However, exaggerating and focusing on the negative aspects of these differences can tug at our sensitivities with a detrimental impact.

We all have some masculine and feminine traits. To avoid sexist behavior that will interfere with our love relationship, we can modify our own approach to gender:

- Be sensitive about sexist remarks when we speak and let others know we do not appreciate hearing such comments.
- Understand that because of differences between genders, and even within the same gender, our partner will be more capable than us in some ways and less capable in other ways. Accept and embrace these differences.
- Women should get in touch with the masculine side of their personality; men should get in touch with the feminine side. When a conflict arises, we will then be more likely to empathize with the opposite sex.

Sustaining Your Snuggle

How do you and your partner feel regarding comments or jokes made about people when the intention is for humor yet the remarks are derogatory? Together, discuss your thoughts on this matter. It is important to understand and respect each other's sensitivities.

Work together to appreciate and accept the differences between you and your partner that may be caused by gender differences. Embrace the masculine and feminine qualities you both share.

Don't Change Who I Am

BETH: Dan, please put on a nicer shirt. It's a formal party for our friends, and it's their tenth anniversary. They're having fifty people, with dancing.

DAN: What's wrong with this shirt? So it has a little stain.

BETH: It's an everyday shirt you wear for work. And I can see the stain from across the room.

DAN: Beth, this is who you married. My choice of clothes has never been an issue for me. Why do you care? I can't change my shirt; it'll mean I'm changing who I am.

BETH: It may not bother you, but it will definitely bother me and everyone else at the party.

DAN: Look, a leopard can't change his spots, and that's what you're asking me to do. I'm a laid-back kinda guy.

BETH: Yeah, if you were any more laid-back, you'd fall backwards on your butt.

The Road to Power Snuggling

Dan tells Beth that changing his shirt will mean changing who he is. We say, "Au contraire!" Certainly, we do not want to sacrifice who we are, but changing behavior does not mean changing our basic personality. We can grow in positive ways without giving up our core values and beliefs.

Living with our partner provides us opportunities to grow, enhancing our strengths and developing new traits. These opportunities for positive growth emerge quite naturally during the course of a partnership as we adjust our behavior to conform to changing circumstances and look for ways to please our partner. In the best-case scenario, some of our partner's admirable characteristics will rub off on us and vice versa.

At times, change may feel threatening. We may fear that our partner is trying to alter our personality. Rather than perceiving our partner as a threat when they make a suggestion for change, we should embrace their request by considering how their can idea can bring improvement to ourselves or a situation. We should also look for ways to compromise. When we realize our partner's suggestion is not an attack on us, but a frustration with something we are doing or not doing, it is easier to hear them out. Our willingness to make the change will please our partner, who in turn will want to return the favor. In a love partnership, we need to continually be open to behavioral changes that will improve our relationship.

Sustaining Your Snuggle

When your partner requests a change in your behavior, do you ever think, "No way can I do that! That's not me"? Do you quietly fret, "It's happening again. They are still trying to change who I am"? Before declining your partner's request, consider their intention and the outcome they desire. Ask yourself if you can accommodate their request as they have proposed or if there is a compromise that you both would find acceptable. Visualize the outcome of this change. Consider that making this alternation will ensure that your partner feels acknowledged and important.

When you realize you are not giving up your core beliefs, but simply adapting to your partner's needs as best you can, you will begin to envision this give-and-take process as a win-win adventure with your lifelong partner.

Say Something!

ALLISON: What did you think of the movie?

LEE: It was okay. I enjoyed it.

ALLISON: Is that all you can say? I thought it was one of the best movies I've ever seen. The lead actors were so, so believable, and the scenery was beautiful. And that little dog reminded me of your mom's dog. C'mon, what did you *really* think of it?

LEE: I told you. I enjoyed it.

ALLISON: Lee, I get so frustrated when you don't talk to me. Maybe you didn't like it because they used that same line a lot.

LEE: You always want me to tell you all my inner thoughts. I don't go on and on yak-yak-yakking. I think to myself. I don't blab everything that pops into my mind.

ALLISON: Oh, so you think I blab? Huh? I don't blab! I offer my feelings. You keep everything inside all the time so nobody knows what you're thinking.

The Road to Power Snuggling

In his book *Keeping the Love You Find,* Dr. Harville Hendrix, founder of Imago Relationship Therapy, explains that most couples include both a "Maximizer" and a "Minimizer." The former is more expressive, while the latter is more reserved. We tend to select a partner whose style is opposite from our own. Maximizers and Minimizers operate differently and are easily identified.

Maximizer	Minimizer
Expresses their feelings openly and desires more conversation in return.	Reluctant to express their feelings.
Becomes frustrated when their partner is not more forthcoming.	Wishes their partner would allow them to experience their thoughts and emotions in peace.

Both styles have power in a relationship, but they use it differently.

The Maximizer often tells their partner what to do. The Minimizer looks for control by agreeing selectively and acting stubborn at times. Often the Maximizer believes the Minimizer lacks emotion because they do not express themselves, but we all have emotions, even when they are not expressed. Imagine a tortoise with its head extended, peacefully basking in the sun. Suddenly the sky darkens, and it starts to hail. The tortoise quickly pulls its head into the safety of its shell. This is how the Minimizer feels when they are bombarded by their energetic, talkative partner, the Maximizer.

To ease tensions, partners must allow each other room for expression. The Maximizer should hold back, allowing the Minimizer to express themselves. The Minimizer needs to be more assertive and share their thoughts and feelings. We should be patient with this process and respect each other's style, understanding that our partner will not become what we are, but they will make progress in our direction.

Sustaining Your Snuggle

As the Maximizer, learn to adjust to your partner's communication style and pace. You may have to wait for a response and later give them a gentle nudge. If you are the Minimizer, take the leap forward and acknowledge your partner's questions or concerns without delay. Initiate conversation. Trust your partner with shared thoughts and feelings. As you apply these new skills, notice a pleasant shift while supporting each other's needs.

Priorities, Priorities

Jack Benny was an American comedian widely regarded as one of the greatest entertainers of his era for his vaudevillian, radio, TV, and film career. He perfected the character of a comic, penny-pinching miser, which he portrayed throughout his forty years on radio and television. The following skit from a 1948 episode of The Jack Benny Program was attributed with receiving one of the longest recorded laughs from a live radio audience.

> (*Benny is returning home when he is accosted by a man with a gun.*)
> MAN: Don't make a move! This is a stickup! . . . Now, come on. Your money or your life!
> (*Benny is silent. Knowing his cheapskate character, the audience begins to laugh.*)
> MAN: Look, bud! I said, "Your money or your life!"
> BENNY: I'm thinking it over!
> (*The audience's laughter goes on for quite some time.*)

The Road to Power Snuggling

Like Jack Benny, we sometimes attach too much importance to particular issues. We argue over matters that seem vital at the time, yet later we cannot recall what the disagreement was about. Accumulation of arguments over small issues can cause great resentment.

We will not always share our partner's priorities, and we can count on the fact that differences of opinion will arise. We should, however, do our best to accommodate concerns that our partner finds significant, whether or not we agree. The following are examples of ways we can bend:

- If our partner feels it is important to clean the kitchen immediately after meals, we should offer our help, even if we think it can wait until later.
- Occasionally we can go to a movie that would not have been our choice, because our partner wants to see that movie and they love having our company.

• We can show patience when our partner needs some extra time to get out of the house.

In order to prevent conflicts, we should accept small differences in priorities without complaints or resentment. Of course there are times when we are not willing to prioritize as our partner would; however, accommodating each other's desires when possible can reap great rewards. Lasting love is usually not about the big issues such as where to live. It is more about pleasing each other during dozens of daily interactions and avoiding bickering. When we acknowledge and agree to our partner's choices, they will feel appreciated with a desire to consider our priorities as well.

Sustaining Your Snuggle

Jack Benny's skit illustrates an extreme choice of priorities. If priorities wreak havoc in your relationship, consider the fallout from continually arguing over these issues. Are your priorities worth risking a loving relationship?

Priorities are an important part of daily life and a means to accomplish what you feel is necessary. However, many people take better care of their prized possessions, such as a car or a home, than they do of their marriage. Certainly you want to hold strong to your principles, but even these change over time. Think of ways you are able to bend to please your partner. Make your marriage your top priority. Your children will also benefit from parents who live in harmony.

Let Your Pet Settle Your Quarrels

At the end of her work day, Donna calls Vern at work:

DONNA: On your way home, would you pick up some milk and get some pizza for dinner?
VERN: Why me? You're closer to the grocery store. And besides, I have another half-hour of work.
DONNA: Look, Vern, I'm always doing the shopping. I've got to get home to let Snooky out. Why can't you get the stuff for a change? Oh, we also need some fruit.

The conversation continues longer than it should have, but Vern finally agrees to buy the groceries.

When Donna arrives home, Snooky jumps up and licks her on the nose. Donna embraces Snooky, speaks to her affectionately in that special baby voice, and then takes her for a walk. She tosses a stick, and Snooky retrieves it, wagging her tail for extra throws.

Back in the house, Donna sips her chamomile tea and strokes Snooky's white, fluffy fur. She thinks back to the conversation she had with Vern and how they were abrupt with each other. She has trouble remembering why their argument began. When Vern returns home, Snooky does her usual thing, excitedly running around in circles and yapping away. The three of them hug.

The Road to Power Snuggling

A study at the State University of New York in Buffalo reveals that couples with pets have closer relationships, and they are more satisfied in their marriages than those who do not have pets. Anna Katzman, one of the researchers, found that the type of pet, whether it is a dog, cat, parakeet, or even fish, does not matter. Pets, according to the study, reduce stress between partners and help nurture social interaction. Pets are attentive and loyal, and they trigger positive memories. They also help us relax. We are all animals, and we are drawn to nature. Pets are nature on demand.

Another study, by Suzanne B. Phillips of Long Island University, shows how pets teach us about our relationship with our love partner. She notes that although couples may vehemently disagree on many topics, they always agree that their dog, cat, horse, or bird is wonderful. Dr. Phillips says that we describe our pets as undemanding, but pets actually require considerable time and attention. They may need special foods, they wreck the furniture, they steal food from countertops, and they pee on the rug. Yet we accept their flaws, and we are quick to forgive because they are cute and we love them dearly.

During a couple's first visit to our therapy office, when we ask our clients about their immediate family, we routinely ask, "Do you have any pets?" The question often generates smiles and giggles. Animals instinctively enjoy and foster a warm, cozy environment at home. On the other hand, pets can sense tension and show their discomfort when people argue or when there is unspoken stress. If their master is in distress, a dog will stay with them for hours until they recover.

Our pets give us unconditional love. If we yell at our dog for barking too much, they will cower and walk away, tail between their legs. Minutes later, all is forgotten and we are best friends again. We do not have to wait for hours, days, or weeks before they recover from a grudge. Pets are not suited for everyone, yet we are on the right track if we learn from them and let love and emotion outshine grievances with our partner.

Sustaining Your Snuggle

You can learn from your pet's unconditional love. They understand that you trust them, and they trust you. Their easygoing approach puts small differences and disagreements in perspective. Notice how pet owners continue to accept and love their pets with compassion regardless of their faults and the attention they require. Owners accept them without judgment or expectation.

People slip up at times, make mistakes, and feel grumpy, stressed, or exhausted. Long-term happiness requires that you find ways to accept your partner's faults and annoyances. Ask yourself if a particular problem really matters in the overall scheme of things. Let your compassion flow, and focus on forgiving as soon as possible, as you would with your pet.

Melting Stress

STEPHANIE: Ricardo, stop nagging me. I know you want me to go looking for new bikes, but I'm on deadline with this paper for work. You know there *are* priorities.

RICARDO: Look, I understand that you have work to do. It seems every weekend you bring work home. I thought you could take a break and do something else. I have a list a mile high of stuff I want to do this weekend, but sometimes we need a change of pace.

STEPHANIE: I guess you're OK mixing activities up and taking breaks. But I'm worried that I won't have this paper ready for the seminar on Monday. Right now I feel overwhelmed with way too much, and your nagging just adds to my stress!

RICARDO: Fine, I'll leave you alone. But it really bugs me that we don't fit in a few moments of fun once in a while.

The Road to Power Snuggling

Our lives are constantly bombarded by people and events. We try to avoid problems and grab at ways to enjoy ourselves. Often we go too far in our quest for pleasure. We often think, "If only things were different. If only my partner understood me better. If only my children behaved or were smarter. If only my boss were nicer. If only I had money to buy that car I want." The media emphasizes what we should purchase to be happier, how to find ways to succeed in life, how we can improve our appearance to feel better about ourselves, and where to go on vacation. We tend to look outside ourselves for ways to make things right, rather than checking in with our conscience. We are frequently disappointed. The result is anxiety, tension, and frustration.

In her book *Everyday Zen*, Charlotte Joko Beck writes, "My dog doesn't worry about the meaning of life. She may worry if she doesn't get her breakfast, but she doesn't sit around worrying about whether she will get fulfilled or liberated or enlightened . . . But we human beings are not like dogs. We have self-centered minds which get us into plenty of trouble" ([San Francisco: Harper Collins, 1989], 3). Another way to look at living,

132

says Beck, is to look inside ourselves by practicing the thousand-year-old tradition of Zen. No, we do not have to give up all we have or stop everything we are doing. There is no need for a special room or adhering to specific positions for meditation, which can also be referred to as "mindfulness." We need only take a few minutes each day to provide ourselves with the gift of solitude and accept what is instead of fighting for change. Zen is about taking in the moment rather than worrying about the past or the future.

Even though this activity is conducted alone, it can have a major impact on our relationship. When we are stressed, our body feels drained, with little energy for anyone else. As we become relaxed and positive, we are more able to focus on our partner and their needs.

In addition to solitary mindfulness, we can find ways to seek peacefulness with our partner. Taking walks in the park and quietly listening to music together will give us moments of calm. We do not need to converse. Instead, we can focus on just being together.

Sustaining Your Snuggle

These are simple steps to give you daily relief from stress. When you are feeling anxious or waiting for a phone call or a traffic light to change, or you are beginning to worry about what you are now worrying about—Stop!

Relax your jaw . . . wait a few seconds.

Relax your arms, then your legs . . . wait a few seconds.

Focus your mind on your breathing, allowing yourself to breathe normally.

Inhale and exhale, counting each breath five times.

Repeat until you are fully relaxed.

You have just meditated and practiced mindfulness. You can reclaim calm by meditating several times a day or for a longer period of time for greater benefits; however, even a few minutes at a time will relax you.

There are many ways of practicing mindfulness. The example provided offers a simple way to calm your nerves. Use this exercise daily for a week and it will become a habit. When your partner indirectly experiences these positive results, they may join you, seeking their own quiet focused time, resulting in a warmer relationship for both parties.

VII

The Enigma of Love

The information included in the following Snuggles may surprise you. We tell you that your relationship will often improve if you act contrary to your instincts. We tell you that winning is losing, that you should avoid the Golden Rule, and that you do not have to say "I love you." Yes, love is a puzzlement. Solving the puzzle requires insight and understanding as you follow the ebb and flow of your relationship on your path to a vibrant and lasting love.

Avoid the Golden Rule to Improve Your Relationship

Sarah decides she will host a surprise party for Ryan's birthday. She spends weeks planning and shopping for just the right foods. She bakes and decorates a birthday cake. She arranges for his best friend to take him to the computer store and bring him back to the house just after the guests have arrived.

After the party, once their friends have left, Sarah asks Ryan about his surprise.

SARAH: You didn't seem very pleased.
RYAN: I said, "Thank you," didn't I?
SARAH: So you were really happy with the party?
RYAN: To tell you the truth, I would have loved to have spent the day playing golf with my buddies and then dining in a quiet restaurant with you in the evening.

The Road to Power Snuggling

The Golden Rule states, "Do unto others as you would have them do unto you." It sounds like a sure bet for improving your relationship. But is it? Sarah followed the Golden Rule. She would have loved it if Ryan had thrown a surprise party for her. But had she followed what we call the "Platinum Rule"—do unto others as they would have you do unto them— Ryan would have been delighted to spend the day golfing with friends and later enjoying a quiet dinner with Sarah.

When we want to please our partner, our first inclination might be to do something that we think they will like because we like it. We are taught to use the Golden Rule as a surefire way to treat everyone. The presumption is that preferences are universal.

We say to our partner, "How can you not like that sofa? I was sure you'd love it." We might be thinking that the fabric in that sofa is durable, and the colors are amazing. However, our partner may prefer two comfortable upholstered chairs with neutral colors.

We might tell our partner, "I can't believe you don't like this delicious chicken dish. I know you love chicken, so I used this new recipe just for you." We may be thinking that it has wonderful spices that make it so tasty. What's not to like? However, our partner would have preferred chicken with plain barbeque sauce.

We wish others would have the same values, desires, and tastes that we enjoy. Later, we realize that many of our choices are not to our partner's liking. Even after years together, couples frequently don't have a clue about their partner's preferences. Dale Carnegie wrote **How to Win Friends and Influence People** in 1936. It has sold more than 15 million copies and has been translated into 31 languages. Carnegie says in his book, "I am very fond of strawberries. But when I go fishing I don't bait the hook with strawberries and cream. Rather, I dangle a worm" ([Pocket Books], 32). Carnegie understands that we will not catch anything if the fish do not like the bait. Likewise, in life we must understand and work within our partner's preferences. We should follow the Platinum rule whether we are fishing or in a loving relationship.

Of course, we cannot disregard the Golden Rule. It works well when we have the same likes and dislikes. But even our understanding of what is kind or unkind will sometimes differ. Maintaining a loving relationship involves focusing on the Platinum Rule by keying into what our partner prefers.

Sustaining Your Snuggle

With your partner, talk about the times when you each used the Golden Rule and the reasons it backfired. How would the results have been different if you had followed the Platinum Rule? Discuss instances in which your tastes are the same and how they differ. Use this new strategy and enjoy the results. Treat your partner to something you know they love, even though it is not your cup of tea or glass of wine.

When Being Right Is Wrong

Patrick and Crystal are visiting Jill and Joel. Patrick is describing their trip to Paris:

PATRICK: So we walked into this fancy restaurant, and I couldn't believe my eyes! At the next table, this woman was holding a monkey in her arms. It was dressed in this red outfit with a little red hat.

CRYSTAL: Wait, it was actually a man who held the monkey, and it was an orange outfit. I remember because it matched your orange shirt.

PATRICK: Whatever. Anyway, we had just been to a restaurant that allowed dogs inside. There's nothing unusual about that in Europe, but seeing a monkey was really weird. Later that day, we went to the Tuileries Garden, where children were guiding their toy boats in the ponds. The setting was beautiful.

CRYSTAL: Patrick, you have a short memory. It wasn't that beautiful. It was raining off and on. Remember, we spent all that time trying to find a place to buy umbrellas?

PATRICK: Anyway, it was great being in Paris in April.

JOEL: Did you get to the Louvre?

PATRICK: Sure did. Spent two full days there. Of course it's an enormous collection, but we did manage to see the *Mona Lisa.*

CRYSTAL: You left out the best part, Honey.

JILL: What's that?

CRYSTAL: The street fair. It was fun bargaining in our Berlitz French. You should've heard Patrick trying to act like he wasn't from Philadelphia. (*Patrick glares at Crystal, purses his lips, and looks down.*)

PATRICK: We'd better go. It's getting late.

After they leave, Jill and Joel hear them arguing outside.

The Road to Power Snuggling

At times we want to offer our partner helpful criticism yet these remarks should be private. Frequent correcting in front of others is a sure way to cool our relationship. The subtle and not-so-subtle criticisms cause resentment. Our partner feels devalued.

Why do we correct our partner in front of others? We might want to politely point out inaccuracies. We may feel competitive and need to set things straight. Or sometimes we feel like teasing. Whatever the reason, we should find ways to avoid criticizing.

Sustaining Your Snuggle

Have there been times when you or your partner felt criticized in the presence of others? How did you react? How did your partner react? When this occurs, discuss your feelings privately. Patrick could have later said, "I was enjoying myself telling them about our Paris trip. Then I was interrupted with corrections. It ruined our conversation, making everyone uncomfortable. Next time, please save your criticisms for our private times." Crystal should then validate Patrick's concern by showing she understands his humiliation and she will no longer criticize him in the presence of others. Discussing the situation calmly allows Patrick to voice his concerns so Crystal can understand why he is upset. It sets the tone for more effective dialog in future situations.

But I Thought He Was the Perfect Guy!

JESSICA: After three months of dating, I've decided to break up with Phil.
SHERRY: You're kidding! Phil? I thought he was perfect. He's so intelligent and good-looking. He's sexy too!
JESSICA: I can't argue with all of that.
SHERRY: And he has a great sense of humor and a good job.
JESSICA: That's all true.
SHERRY: So what's the problem?
JESSICA: When I first met him, I thought he had everything. But I now realize that he doesn't have the one thing I need most.
SHERRY: What's that?
JESSICA: He's not kind.
SHERRY: No? He buys you presents. Takes you to shows.
JESSICA: Yeah, that's generous, but it's not what I'd call kind. Remember when my dog died? All he said was, "I'll get you another dog." When I told him about my sister's problem, he said, "Well, that's not your problem, so forget it." Now that I've known him for awhile, I've seen him get nasty with his neighbors and impatient with a brother who's having issues. What really bothers me is that he can't seem to key into how I feel either.

The Road to Power Snuggling

The significance of compassion in a relationship cannot be overstated. David M. Buss of the University of Texas analyzed the relationship choices of individuals from 37 different cultures. Ranking thirteen different factors, he found the most important mate selection factor for both men and women is how kind a person is. Kindness ranked first, way above earning capacity or religious orientation.

Jessica comes to the same conclusion about the importance of compassion during her time with Phil. Although his other qualities are certainly desirable, Jessica feels that he is insensitive. For her, the empathy that is missing trumps Phil's good looks and all his gifts. Without that essential ingredient, their relationship feels empty to her.

Evidence indicates that the more someone witnesses kindness, the more they will be kind themselves. Consider the implications of this cycle of compassion in your love relationship. A single considerate act will lead to ever-increasing levels of kindness between you and your partner.

Sustaining Your Snuggle

Mark Twain once said, "Kindness is the language which the deaf can hear and the blind can see." How can you demonstrate this powerful and vital trait in your own relationship? Kindness means empathizing with your partner, even when you do not feel the way they do. Kindness means being careful not to embarrass your partner in front of others. It means showing your partner that you care for others who have problems. It means being available when your partner needs you, both to listen and to empathize.

You Don't Have to Say "I Love You" to Say I Love You

David and Michelle are eating in a café. This is their eighth date in six weeks:

DAVID: (*Looks at Michelle, smiles, and pats her hand.*)
MICHELLE: (*Returns David's smile and then coyly turns away.*)
DAVID: (*Quietly bites a Danish pastry while he focuses on her eyes.*)
MICHELLE: (*Reaches out and takes the Danish from his hand, quickly taking a bite, and gives it back. She giggles.*)

The Road to Power Snuggling

In every social contact we determine whether someone cares about us by reading their tiniest facial expressions, the tone of their words, eye contact or lack thereof, and body motions. We also make judgments based on the presence or absence of special deeds, such as giving a love poem. Over time, we learn to communicate with nonverbal messages, hopefully in more positive than negative ways. A UCLA study concluded that 93 percent of communication effectiveness is determined by nonverbal cues. Though other researchers differ as to whether that figure should be 60 percent, or somewhere in between, they agree that nonverbal communication is critical to all relationships.

In *Fiddler on the Roof* (score by Jerry Bock and Sheldon Harnick), Tevye asks his wife, Golde, "Do you love me?" She sings, "After twenty-five years I've washed your clothes, cooked your meals . . . milked the cows. . . . I suppose I do." And he sings, "I suppose I love you, too." Most of us need more than Golde and Tevye's "I suppose I do." We deserve direct and regular refueling of committed love. We receive this through both verbal and, just as importantly, nonverbal language. And we need it *now*, not after twenty-five years.

Sustaining Your Snuggle

We each differ as to what makes us feel loved, but positive nonverbal communication skills help your relationship flourish. There are those who feel most loved when they receive gifts. Some like their partner to carry out their chores. Others like a night on the town. Most of us want a combination of these. Try the following nonverbal ways to communicate your love:

- Leave a loving note on the bathroom mirror.
- Look at your partner emphatically when they are telling you about a problem.
- Hand your partner the TV remote.
- Eat dinner with dimmed lights and play your partner's favorite music.
- Let your partner sleep in on the weekend.
- Wash the dishes when it is not your turn.
- Light candles in the bedroom.
- Provide loving smiles.

With your partner, discuss the nonverbal behavior that makes each of you feel most loved. Provide these treats.

What Makes a Happy Marriage?

Which of the following couples is more likely to have a happier marriage?

Susan and Will

Susan and Will meet at a ski resort. Both are outgoing and have a great sense of humor. Susan is a lawyer, specializing in health law. Will is a healthcare economist. They grew up within a few miles of each other near Providence. They both enjoy collecting modern paintings. They talk up a storm until 3 A.M.

Erica and Todd

Erica and Todd meet in a grocery store. Todd is shopping for ingredients to cook a gourmet dinner. Erica has only cooked basic meals. She volunteers at the local animal shelter. Todd always wanted a dog but has never had one. He is an award-winning author. Erica teaches ballet. Todd invites her to join him and his friends for dinner that night.

We cannot be sure which couple will be happier, but research indicates that the outlook is brighter for Erica and Todd. Why? Erica and Todd bring their diverse and unique personalities, talents, and interests into the relationship and expand the other's life by integrating these qualities into their life together. Studies show that experiencing this "self-expansion" from one's partner is key to a committed and satisfying long-term relationship.

Couples benefit most when they are encouraged by their partner to grow in new ways, thus realizing their own talents and potential. Because of their differences, Erica and Todd have the potential to make each other's life more exciting. Of course, they each have to want to learn from the other. Susan and Will can do the same, but since they began their relationship with similar personalities and interests, they may have to work harder to stimulate each other's growth.

The Road to Power Snuggling

When we fall in love, we quickly experience self-expansion with this new and exciting person. We each try on different roles as we begin the romance. Over time our personal development becomes more subtle. However, differences—rather than similarities—provide the spark, along with the challenges, that sustain a long-term, happy relationship.

By examining each other's strengths and interests, we can find stimulating growth areas for both of us. One of us may be more outgoing and the other more pensive; one may be more creative and the other more practical. These distinctions provide a recipe for growth by providing us the opportunities to learn about and admire the abilities of the other. Though there are other factors that lead to happy marriages, taking advantage of our differences is a great starting point.

Sustaining Your Snuggle

What talents do you admire most in your partner? How are their interests different from your own? When you notice a characteristic or interest that is appealing, do you allow yourself access into this new realm?

Enliven your time together by capitalizing on the benefits of your differences. Your life will become more fulfilling as you learn to spice it up with the lure of your individualities coming together as a twosome.

If You Win, You Both Lose

JASON: I hope we get home before it gets dark. I don't like driving after dark.

TRACY, *looking at the map*: Here's an interesting fact. Did you know we live east of Reno, Nevada?

JASON: What? Tracy, you're crazy! There's no way L.A. is east of Reno. You know we live near the ocean, so how can we be east of Reno? We're way west of Reno.

TRACY: You never trust me. I saw it on the map. And don't call me crazy.

(*Tracy flips her hair, almost hitting Jason in the face as he drives.*)

JASON: No way, no how. What you're telling me makes no sense, Tracy.

TRACY: I feel like I always have to prove everything to you, Mr. Know-It-All. You never believe me. You always think you're so right.

It is going to be a long, tense drive home. If Jason and Tracy overheard a similar conversation between strangers, they would have opinions about who is right, but they would not feel the same strong emotions they experienced in the car. What causes these outbursts?

The Road to Power Snuggling

When we feel we are right and our point of view is being dismissed, we push our ideas onto the other, and the discussion is no longer a discussion. It quickly shifts into a debate and sometimes an argument. This causes hurt feelings. Being right builds our ego but deflates our partner. They will feel resentful when their judgment is questioned after presenting their case with all their energy. When these types of arguments become a way of life, no one wins. We both seek new strategies to prove we are smarter. With increased resentment, the arguments set the stage for resorting to blame whenever there is a problem.

As in a work or classroom setting, which requires cooperative problem solving, it is very satisfying when we brainstorm together to resolve an issue, truly considering each other's ideas. When we know we will have the opportunity to speak our mind, explaining our position and our concerns, we can take a deep breath and fully listen to our partner's perspective on the issue. Acknowledging differences and being open to new ideas will help us come to a peaceful resolution.

Jason and Tracy's disagreement could have been resolved peacefully:

JASON, *incredulous:* Really? You say L.A. is east of Reno? How's that possible if L.A. is on the Pacific Coast?

TRACY: Yep. That's right. Most of California is west of Nevada, but the map shows L.A. east of Reno.

JASON: I guess, but it's really weird. Let's check the map when we stop for lunch. (*They stop to check the map and Jason finds that Los Angeles is indeed east of Reno. He admits his mistake and offers Tracy a smile.*)

There is a correct answer to Tracy and Jason's debate, but many disagreements are not as factually clear-cut and involve judgment calls. In such cases, we must discuss our opinions without belittling our partner. For instance, if we believe a movie was wonderful and our partner thinks it was terrible, we might be tempted to consult the movie's reviews to build our case. But checking reviews for opinions does not give us a right or wrong answer since this discussion is really about preferences, not facts. Allowing our partner to express their own opinions while we withhold judgment of their views goes a long way to fostering peace and trust in a relationship.

Sustaining Your Snuggle

When you disagree about facts, check the information in a noncombative way. If the disagreement involves different values or tastes, such as whether a movie or type of food is outstanding or unpalatable, describe what pleases or displeases you. You will not agree on all issues. That isn't human nature. However, respecting and even admiring your differences will add excitement to your relationship and bring you closer.

Think of how a recent argument could have been peacefully resolved, without a winner or a loser. When another issue arises, be prepared to calmly listen to each other's point of view with the goal of coming together without blame. The result will be more satisfying and less stressful.

You Met Your Partner by Chance, Didn't You?

How can ten seconds change your life? In the 1998 movie *Sliding Doors*, Helen Quilley runs down the stairs of a London Underground station. She arrives on the platform just in time to catch the train. In a second sequence, Helen is again running down the stairs. This time, a young girl with a doll delays her progress by ten seconds. The train doors close just before she can board. The movie alternates between Helen's two parallel lives. One version follows Helen's life after she catches the first train. The other follows her very different life and relationships after she boards the second train.

The Road to Power Snuggling

Remember how you and your partner met? You met by chance, didn't you? You might have been assigned to the same class in school or worked in the same office. You might have been introduced by a friend or happened to attend the same party. You might have bumped into each other on a plane or while out shopping. What slight variation in your life or your partner's life might have occurred to prevent you from ever meeting? Despite the various possibilities, somehow you did meet, and you followed through, both deciding to continue your relationship.

With our partner we are often presented with our own daily version of *Sliding Doors*. The good news is that we can choose which course we want our lives to take. Whether or not we open a particular "door" to foster our relationship can play a major role in our emotional and physical well-being. We should consider the doors that could open wider if we choose to say or do something that will bring us closer. We also need to be aware of the doors that could close if we choose to say or do something that causes discomfort.

Sustaining Your Snuggle

Power Snuggling requires taking action, regardless of whether you happen to catch the first or the second train. If one door does not lead where you would like, choose another one. Behind every door, there are exciting opportunities within your relationship waiting for you. Find them and open them.

Unfair Games

BRENDA, *walking toward the car:* You know, Richard, our house needs painting. (*She thinks, "I've been asking him for months. I wonder if he loves me enough to take care of it."*)

RICHARD: I've told you, we're tight on funds. You know we can't afford to paint the house now. (*He thinks, "She keeps bugging me. If she really loves me, she'll understand that I'm doing my best to make ends meet."*)

BRENDA: Well, it's been years since the house was painted, and it looks terrible. (*She thinks, "I'll give him another chance to let me know he loves me."*)

RICHARD: I'm tired of listening to this. Why don't you go to the movies alone? (*He thinks, "If she really loves me, she'll get off this topic. She won't really go alone."*)

Brenda: Fine, I'll do just that! (*She thinks, "That proves he doesn't love me. There's no way I'm going to be with someone who doesn't love me."*)

(*Richard thinks, "Obviously, she couldn't care less about what I think. That shows where I stand."*)

Although Brenda really wants the house painted and Richard is worried about money, their conversation is not truly about painting the house and money. It is more about emotional tugs and determining how much each is willing to sacrifice for the other as a way to confirm their love.

The Road to Power Snuggling

In 1964, Eric Berne wrote the best-selling book *Games People Play* in which he describes how our strong desire to be loved leads us to converse in ways which we feel increase our importance and power. Although Berne describes these Power Struggles as "games," they are not fun. They are contrived situations that are substitutes for real living and intimacy. Berne notes that every game is basically dishonest with dramatic outcomes. In Brenda and Richard's game, their indirect message to each other is "If you really love and respect me, you will cater to all my desires." Another example of a game is "If it weren't for you," in which one partner tries to blame the other for not accomplishing something. For example, "If it weren't for you, I would have studied and learned French, but you demanded too much of my time." These so-called games reduce trust, hurt feelings, and damage our relationship.

Real connection and intimacy means we avoid games and speak with our true feelings. Instead of testing our partner's love, we need to take a closer look at what they have said and done over time to exhibit love. We need to be conscious of the truth of our relationship and the love that fuels it. In a conscious relationship, love is not tested; it is accepted. Just because our partner will not agree to take care of our every desire does not mean that love is absent.

If Brenda and Richard know that the other loves them, their actions are likely to support each other. In a conscious relationship, Brenda would not have mentioned house painting at this inopportune time as a means of making Richard prove his love for her. Had she slipped by telling Richard the house needed painting, she would have quickly dropped the subject and not ruined their movie plans. In a conscious relationship, Richard would have respected Brenda's desires and acknowledged that the house does need painting. He would have agreed to discuss the issue later. Using this example, couples can move from testing love to assuming love and helping it grow.

Sustaining Your Snuggle

To return to an intimate relationship, be conscious of the games that each of you initiate. If your partner begins a game, look for a way to avoid entering the fray. If you find you are initiating a game, look for a way to quickly defuse it.

If you discover that you are repeating the same games, realize that each of you needs more "stroking." Berne uses the word "stroking" as a term for intimate contact, whether it be loving words or a hug. As you recognize what is occurring, and as you provide more and more daily strokes, these damaging games will fade. You will then be on your way to the intimate and safe relationship you deserve.

Being Together yet Feeling Alone

Valerie is confessing to her sister, Maggie.

VALERIE: Something's definitely wrong. I can't believe relationships are meant to be like this. We've been together for nearly three years, but I don't feel we're together. Oh, we sometimes go to movies, hang out with a few mutual friends, and make love, but I feel like I'm alone in our house even when he's there. Do you feel that way with Don?

MAGGIE: Not really. Sure, when things aren't going well I'll have moments of loneliness. But usually we enjoy doing things together. Even when we're home engaged in our own activities, we feel each other's presence and check up on each other. Valerie, you need to do something about your situation. Don't let it go on like that for years.

The Road to Power Snuggling

Picture a couple sitting in a restaurant staring blankly away from each other. When their waiter arrives, he suggests, "It's not on the menu, but I could offer you something to talk about." As Valerie has discovered, many committed couples find themselves drifting apart. These couples may live in the same house yet live parallel lives, each feeling quite lonely. They go about their days and their lives as separate from their partner, pursuing their own interests and friendships, sheltering their thoughts and emotions, and neglecting those of their partner. This causes frustration, frequent quarrels that end without compromise, and a continual feeling of disconnect and loneliness.

To reunite, couples must decide to work together. A meaningful relationship requires that couples listen to each other intently, understand the other's problems, and participate in some activities together. According to a comprehensive study of the marriages of more than two thousand married people, conducted between 1980 and 2000, the likelihood of couples participating together in recreational activities fell by 28 percent during the course of their marriage. Considering the explosion of electronic communication since 2000, it is likely that couples today spend even less time together. They may even exchange emails while in adjoining rooms, avoiding conversation. Sure, that's efficient, but emails and texts do not substitute for a close, emotional companionship.

Sustaining Your Snuggle

If you feel that what you say never reaches your partner and you frequently move in different directions, the chances are your partner also feels this disconnect. It is time to make changes. To switch from a couple on survival mode and move into a warm partnership, find a peaceful time to plan changes. Each partner should make a list of activities you would like to enjoy together and write them in the present tense, as if you are already engaged in them. By using the present tense, you are encouraged to move ahead quickly. You might write, "We go biking together often. We see movies together. We have a date night once a week. We get together with friends regularly." Compare your two lists and carry out the activities that interest you both. The anticipation of fun times to come will bring the allure of excitement into your home.

When you have disagreements, be sure to listen intently to each other's ideas and compromise. Cooperating on one issue will lay the foundation for resolving others. Over time you will become more connected and recapture that feeling of togetherness.

It's Never Too Late

Roz and Leo are in a restaurant.

LEO: Look at that couple. Remember when we acted like that?
ROZ: Kind of. It's been so long.
LEO: Look at the way he's smiling at her.
ROZ: I know. And now he's rubbing the back of her hand. That's so sweet.
LEO: See how she's pushing her hair back and winking at him?
ROZ: Didn't I do that too?
LEO: I'm sure you did. You were amazing that way.
ROZ: I remember when you danced out of the movie theater and bowed to me like you were Fred Astaire. Once you even dripped chocolate syrup on my arm and wrote my initial.
LEO: That was fun. Then you started giggling. You know, it's sad but after eight years of marriage and children, we're no longer in that fun and flirty age group. It seems like a lifetime ago since we had that. I wish we were young again. We'd have a blast.

What Roz and Leo do not know is that the couple they are watching in the restaurant, Roger and Gwen, have been married for twelve years and they have a babysitter at home taking care of their four children. Roger and Gwen have been flirting since the day they met. Of course, they have disagreements at times, as do we all. In fact, sometimes they worry about neighbors hearing them during a shouting match. But the high priority they place on the affectionate, loving part of their relationship moves them back into a cozier place once the anger dissipates.

The Road to Power Snuggling

Flirting can be thought of as kidding around, but the intention is to attract one another, to be one with each other, to continue the special "we." When flirting occurs, words are not always needed. Anthropologist David Givens, director of the Center for Nonverbal Studies in Spokane, Washington, and author of *Love Signals,* tells us, "When it comes to emotions, our bodies do the talking more than words" (Paula Spencer Scott, "9 Wordless Ways Someone Says, 'I Love You,'" Caring.com). Givens writes that couples unconsciously mirror each other's actions, strengthening their bond. They show they are approachable by locking eyes, rolling shoulders, tilting their head, and smiling warmly. When we avoid eye contact while our partner is speaking, they know we are not engaged in their dialogue. When we lean toward our partner while they speak and meet their eyes, we imply we want to be closer, and we are interested in what they have to say.

When we first dated, along with our body language we often flirted with innuendos and with tender words that meant something only to us. We exchanged smiles for no reason at all. Unfortunately, we may have stopped flirting when the pressures of daily life began to weigh upon us or as problems in our relationship emerged. It is a challenge for us to move into a loving zone when the chips are down. If we return to our flirtatious ways and build affection into our life, it becomes easier to overcome our relationship problems.

Sustaining Your Snuggle

Flirting is the glue that maintains the emotional closeness between you and your partner. How have you flirted in the past? What emotions do those memories convey? Talk about them and relive those pleasurable times.

You will find that flirting warms your relationship, and it tones down frustrations when there are differences. Behind those frustrations is a feeling of closeness that helps you weather the storms. It is magical rediscovering the joy of each other.

VIII

Taking Steps for Greater Love

Each day we need to seek ways to maintain the good parts of our relationship and expand our love. This is how our relationship will grow deeper and more meaningful.

How Long Should I Wait?

 LaToya disliked her job. No, it was worse than that. She *hated* her job. But it paid well, so for six years, she trudged to the office and even received promotions. Her husband, Christopher, praised her for her success. Since they needed two incomes, she kept working.

At times LaToya imagined having the following conversation with her husband:

> LaToya: You know, Christopher, I really hate working there. Every day I wake up and think what it would be like if I tried something more creative. But I don't know what it would be, and I doubt I could earn as much as I do now.
>
> Christopher: LaToya, you don't mean that, do you? You're so good at it, and I don't know how we'd survive with less money. I really hope you won't let our family down.

Over the months, this imaginary conversation played in LaToya's mind. It became more problematic, as she grew to dislike her job even more. Eventually she realized she couldn't go on as she had been. She decided to let the chips fall where they may and really talk with Christopher. LaToya finally told her husband exactly how she felt. To her surprise, he replied, "LaToya, you really should quit and look for something else. We'll survive. A job shouldn't be unbearable. It may take a while, but I'm sure you'll find something where you can use your creativity."

The Road to Power Snuggling

You may have heard the tale about the farmer who for years plowed around a boulder in his field. He thought it was too large to dig out. Season after season, he drove his plow around the long, flat rock. One day the plow accidentally nicked the stone, and it moved. The farmer jumped from the plow and discovered the rock was large, but it was only a quarter-inch thick. He easily flipped it out of his planting field.

Too often we, as couples, continue an unhappy or dull pattern for years, hoping change will occur by itself. This might mean that out of habit, we keep the same job, never meet new friends or look for new hobbies, and watch the same TV shows. Trying something new will not guarantee us a more interesting life. However, more often than not, a couple's relationship will be stimulated by sharing thoughts and feelings, along with new adventures. The rock in our path might be much easier to move than we think.

Sustaining Your Snuggle

Are there areas of your life that you think need change? Are you comfortable sharing your desires with your partner, or do you feel reluctant because you worry about their response?

Couples often want to take action that impacts both of them, resulting in minor or major adjustments. Take a chance and share some of your concerns. Tell your partner your pie-in-the-sky wishes. Ask them to share their yearnings. Listen. Then brainstorm together, building your hopes together and allowing dreams to emerge.

Build—Don't Steal—Your Partner's Poker Chips

Donna and Jack decided to take advantage of the beautiful weather and plan a spur-of-the-moment picnic. In a secluded spot at their favorite park, they found a table and began to eat lunch.

DONNA: I'm so glad you suggested this. It sure beats driving around running Saturday errands and doing chores.
JACK: Yeah. I figured the chores aren't going anywhere, and I wanted to take advantage of this amazing weather.
DONNA: I love that you do that.
JACK: Do what?
DONNA: That you often look for ways we can have fun together. I love that about you!

The Road to Power Snuggling

We all want to feel good about ourselves. Having our egos stroked by our partner builds our confidence. If our partner admires us, we are energized and more likely to strive for a happy, fulfilling life together.

The thrill we experience when we build up our partner and share in each other's life successes can be compared to winning a hand at poker. When we play poker, we begin with a stack of chips. If we win big—or we succeed alongside our partner—our confidence soars, and we are invigorated, willing to bet more on life and each other since we still have a stack in reserve for future hands. However, if our pile dwindles—or we lack support from our relationship—we are likely to be timid and bet fewer chips, allowing our relationship to fold.

Life can be viewed as the sum of the "chips" we have netted through our struggles and triumphs. When we were very young, our parents took care of all our needs. They fed us, diapered us, hugged us, and comforted us when we cried. They celebrated with us and encouraged us. And we felt wonderful. We acted like a poker player with a large stack of chips. We took risks and even if we lost our way, we could go back and take more

160

risks because losing a few poker chips still left us with plenty and loads of confidence. This confidence encouraged us to raise our hand in class, experiment with creative activities, and assist less fortunate people.

As we mature, our role in the game changes. We are no longer children freely earning chips and blithely paying the costs because we are assured that our supply will be renewed. Rather, it becomes our responsibility to replenish ourselves and our confidence while looking to help our partner build up their reserves. Over the years, our stack of poker chips, as well as our partner's stack, rises and falls with life's successes and failures. Relationships grow warmer as our two stacks of poker chips grow. Having chips helps us love our partner because we love ourselves. We cannot always control our partner's successes, however. Nevertheless, when we are together, we have the opportunity to change our partner's supply of chips. We increase chips by complimenting our partner. We steal chips by criticizing them. It's a win-win if we help each other build success.

Sustaining Your Snuggle

Think of ways you can increase your partner's stack of poker chips, then do it. At first they may feel awkward listening to your praise. Do not be discouraged. Over time they will soften, enjoying the admiration. Now think of ways you might be stealing your partner's chips. Stop robbing them of their confidence and work together to rebuild your relationship's success.

How to Talk so Your Partner Listens

JESS: Brent, you always leave the car keys where I can't find them. You never hang them up.

BRENT: You know, Jess, you're never satisfied. Big deal about the car keys. You're not so perfect. You always throw my newspapers away before I even read them.

JESS, *rolling her eyes in agitation:* Well, you leave them in a mess, and besides that has nothing to do with car keys. How can I leave the house without keys?

BRENT: If you just look around, you'll find them.

The Road to Power Snuggling

Arguments about the same issues can reemerge for years. Sometimes they cease only when we give up because we believe changes will never occur. Other times partners tune out and walk away, afraid to perpetuate uncomfortable situations. However, both parties will still continue to feel resentment with anger reverberating through the walls of the house. The solution lies not in ignoring the problem but in talking so that our partner can hear us then listening so that our partner can talk.

In the above situation, Jess and Brent need to take four important steps.

- First, Jess, who initiated the discussion, should pick a time to raise this issue when she and Brent are at peace and able to devote time to listening to one another. Brent cannot listen when she is running out the door.
- Second, Jess and Brent both need to change their language. We should toss the words "always" and "never" down the garbage disposal and grind them well. In their place, we need to substitute "I" messages. For example Jess could rephrase her request: "Brent, when I'm ready to leave the house, and I can't find the keys, I get very frustrated. I worry that I'll be late for work. I'd feel much better if the keys are on the hook. I would really appreciate that." Notice

Jess uses the word "I" to show her feelings. If she had used the word "you" instead, her language would have implied blame.

Jess also needs to eliminate negative nonverbal language such as eye-rolling, finger-pointing, shoulder-shrugging, or door-slamming. Negative body language begs the other person to become defensive and then counterattack. Instead, we need to hold our emotions in check and think how we would act at a business meeting when we want results.

- Third, Brent should validate Jess's concern. Brent can say, "I know it's very annoying when you can't find the keys and you're ready to leave for work. It makes sense you would be upset because you're concerned that you'll be late for work." When we validate our partner, we are telling them that we support and recognize their thoughts and feelings. We might say, "From your perspective, I understand why you feel that way." We can take that a step further by saying, "It makes sense you feel that way because . . ." and explain their point of view. Validation does not mean we agree with their statement; however, it means that we agree that they feel the way they do.
- Fourth, when Jess finds the keys on the hook, she should tell Brent, "Thanks for hanging up the keys." A smile and a hug will work wonders.

These four steps really work. If you choose not to use them, you are headed for the fate of Sisyphus, forever trying to push your burden up a hill only to have to face it again when the issue rolls back down.

Sustaining Your Snuggle

You might ask, "Why can't I say what I feel when I feel it? Why do I have to show appreciation for something that my partner is **supposed** to do?" Before expressing strong feelings, think about comments that might hurt or place blame. It is difficult for your partner to listen when anger or other intense emotions are directed towards them. If you express your thoughts in a calm, reasonable, non-threatening way and thank your partner when they meet your desires, you will gain their understanding and trust—even if they are not in agreement.

A Three-Minute Relationship Change

DANIELLE: I had an awful time getting home in that horrible rain. As I left the subway—
KYLE: Why didn't you call me?
DANIELLE: Wait, Kyle. So I got up to the street with no umbrella and—
KYLE: If you couldn't get me, you could have taken a cab.
DANIELLE: Kyle, let me talk. I knew you were still at work, but I tried anyway on your cell. Got no answer. I had no luck trying to flag a taxi, no umbrella, and torrents of—
KYLE: How did you get home?
DANIELLE: This is just too much. Do you have any idea what you're doing? I've had a lousy day that I somehow managed to turn around, and I wanted so much to share it with you. But you constantly interrupt me. How unfair is that?
KYLE: Okay, go ahead.
DANIELLE: Well, I ran across the street, you know, to that pizza place. I ordered a pizza to be delivered to our house. Then I asked if I could ride with them. They said, "Sure."
KYLE: Wow! So you kept dry, and you got a free ride with hot pizza. Way to go!

The Road to Power Snuggling

Even though Kyle is a caring and supportive guy, his constant interruptions and suggestions caused Danielle to feel frustrated and edgy. Ironically, he was trying hard to be helpful by voicing his concern and offering solutions. Danielle could not appreciate his good intentions. Instead, she became angry at his rudeness since he would not give her the time she needed to fully express herself.

Many of our conversations become chopped pieces of sentences. We start talking and try to make our point, but our partner interrupts or looks elsewhere, and our words never reach them. They are already thinking ahead, guessing what we are about to say, then planning what they will say next. Often our partners interrupt us because they want to fix a situation.

Men are blamed more than women for seeking solutions to a problem rather than allowing their partner to express themselves; however, our experience shows both genders share the blame. We know we should just listen and not try to resolve the problem. Yet it seems natural to think of a fix or a rebuttal.

Although the intention behind them may be positive, with frequent interruptions, we feel invalidated, alone, and sometimes invisible. Even when routine conversations are interrupted, it makes it difficult to discuss important issues, because we become distracted knowing we will be interrupted again.

Sustaining Your Snuggle

Listening includes stopping all other activities, maintaining eye contact, and concentrating on your partner's verbal and nonverbal communication. Watch their facial expressions and body language. Are they frustrated? Afraid? Confident? Anxious? Loving? Do you see a combination of these emotions? What is their message? Are they asking something from you or do they just want to share their thoughts with a good listener?

When your partner is finished speaking, take a moment then paraphrase what you heard so they will know you understood. If necessary, ask questions to clarify. This will show that you truly care. Avoid posing questions that begin with "Why didn't you?" or telling them "You should have." These remarks beg a defensive response. Your partner needs to know you are on their side.

The next time your partner has something to say, listen attentively without interruption for at least *three minutes*. Nod or use facial expressions to show you are on board. Your partner will be delighted with the attention, and you will both reap the benefits.

The Impressive Benefits of Sexual Intimacy

TERESA: You really turned me on this morning.
NICK: I'm so glad you suggested we take off work today and have a peaceful—how do I say it?—rendezvous.
TERESA: I think we're both improving with age.
NICK: Practice makes perfect.

The Road to Power Snuggling

What is physical intimacy? Romantic touching, hugging, kissing, holding hands, and sexual activity are all included in the spectrum of physical intimacy. Such affection should not be limited to the bedroom. A healthy love relationship includes frequent touching and physical contact.

What are the benefits? When we welcome a hug or touch or experience other forms of physical intimacy, our body releases one or more of three chemicals: oxytocin, dopamine, and serotonin. These chemicals provide very pleasurable feelings, and they also have a major impact on our physical and mental well-being. Oxytocin increases our desire to bond. Dopamine improves our mood. And serotonin protects us against depression.

Extensive research studies indicate the positive effects of physical affection and sex. The findings show that sex:

- Reduces stress and blood pressure;
- Increases levels of antibodies, reducing our susceptibility to infection;
- Improves our cardiovascular system, reducing our chances of heart attack and stroke;
- Increases confidence and self-esteem;
- Reduces pain (as oxytocin surges, endorphins increase and pain subsides);
- Reduces the risk of prostate cancer;
- Helps us sleep better through the release of oxytocin; and
- Builds trust, improving our long-term relationship.

We have an innate need to feel accepted and to be desired by our love partner. Intimacy is possible when that need is met. We have found in our work with hundreds of couples that hugging and touching, as well as sexual activity, is a vital part of a romantic relationship. In her book, *Hold Me Tight*, Dr. Sue Johnson writes, "When partners are emotionally accessible, responsive, and engaged, sex becomes intimate play, a safe adventure ([New York: Little, Brown and Company, 2008], 186).

Sustaining Your Snuggle

Compromise and planning are required to satisfy both partners' sexual needs. This week, do some soul searching into your own desires and concerns. Then share your thoughts in an open conversation with your partner. The topic of sex may be awkward at first. But it is important to listen to and understand each other's feelings and desires. Fulfilling sexual needs will spread positive vibes into all areas of your relationship.

Let's Talk about Sex

A scene from the movie *Annie Hall* shows Woody Allen as Alvy talking with his psychiatrist. In a split screen, Diane Keaton as the eponymous Annie Hall shares with her own psychiatrist.

PSYCHIATRIST: How many times do you sleep together?
ALVY: Hardly ever, maybe three times a week.

PSYCHIATRIST: Do you have sex often?
ANNIE: Constantly, I'd say three times a week.

Understanding and accepting each other's sexual desires is critical to a love relationship. We may select our partner for many reasons, including security, companionship, and ability to raise a family, but at some point we end up naked in bed together.

The Road to Power Snuggling

Love relationships involve an erotic and sexual connection. Our sexuality is revealed in the way we talk, laugh, joke, touch, dress, or even cook dinner together. We all have our means of expressing sexuality, and each of us connects to our partner in different ways. The physical connection can be amazingly beautiful or humdrum or very uncomfortable. Over time, it is not uncommon to experience all of these.

Sex is a topic that even the closest couples have difficulty discussing, especially when their views and desires are far apart, but being comfortable with our own sensuality/sexuality is key to emotional intimacy with our partner. At the same time, it is important to understand and accept our partner's comfort level: how often, what they like or dislike, and type of sexual experience that pleases them. These factors help assure a close and satisfying relationship.

A frequent source of frustration in long-term love relationships is frequency. Sexual frequency often wanes over time, but most people continue to desire some level of physical intimacy throughout their life, regardless of age. Though men generally desire more sex than women, the reverse can also be true. When sex diminishes or is lost, we often hear, "I feel so hurt that I want him/her to make the first move to reconnect." This imbalance causes one or both partners to feel undesirable, followed by feelings of rejection and resentment. This leads to conflicts that crop up in other areas, leading to emotional and ultimately physical separation. Disconnected partners will search for new outlets such as work, hobbies, or other companions.

What prevents us from continuing at a level of intimacy that satisfies both partners? Intimacy may diminish due to exhaustion with work or the demands of a family, physical ailments, negative body image, or changes in hormone levels. Unfortunately as sex diminishes, many couples are reluctant to discuss the issue. Women, more so than men, say that their feelings are not validated by their partner, making it difficult for them to feel loving and sexual.

Since we all need to be listened to and understood it is essential to keep our line of communication open. When one of us voices our opinion about anything sexual, our partner needs to accept our feelings. When our thoughts are validated, we become more comfortable and willing to discuss and resolve intimacy issues.

Sustaining Your Snuggle

Sex is a vital component of love relationships that deserves at least the same effort of discussion given to other important issues. If either partner believes your sexual relationship is not working, it is time to evaluate your intimacy. When too little or too much sex is causing either of you major problems, your relationship will suffer.

When is the last time either of you initiated a discussion about sex? Before starting a discussion, make sure you are both available and willing to talk. Begin your conversation by agreeing that your goal is to improve both partners' enjoyment of sex. Each of you should state what you enjoy and what may be turning you off. Try using the phrases "I feel most loving when . . ." and "I get turned off when . . . ."

Each of you has different desires so you need to find behaviors that will satisfy both your needs. Respect each other's feelings and preferences. Knowing what your partner desires and what they are willing to try will require less guesswork. This conversation will lead to better understanding and fulfillment, but as with any other topic, compromise is needed.

Learning to Love after Infidelity

Sally is in the backyard chatting with her neighbor, Juanita.

SALLY: Did you hear about Ralph and Rita and his affair?
JUANITA: Uh-huh. Rita was pretty open about it. I've never seen her so upset. She told me she's kicking him out of the house.
SALLY: I guess the marriage is over. I could never live with a man who is disloyal.
JUANITA: I can't imagine Carl cheating on me, but if he did I don't know what I'd do. It's disturbing that affairs are so common these days.
SALLY: You wouldn't split up? I certainly would if Dave did anything like that. How could I ever trust him again?
JUANITA: I'm not sure what I'd do. I guess it would depend on the particulars. It's a difficult choice after being close and living together for so many years.

The Road to Power Snuggling

There are countless studies and articles written about infidelity, with widely differing estimates of the extent of the problem. However, all articles agree that infidelity is a major concern. Affairs are extremely damaging, often to both parties, their children, and extended families. It is very painful when we discover that our partner has been unfaithful. The healing process, if it is to occur, may take years.

After an affair there is a ripple effect in the life of both partners. We see life differently. We may seek a different job, a different house, or a way to end our relationship. The mental suffering which results from a partner having an affair is extensive. The person who has been cheated on suffers a blow to their self-esteem. They may wonder, "Why did I let this happen? Why am I not desired?" After the affair they will find it difficult to trust others. They will harbor feelings of instability, and emotions may range from sadness to helplessness to anger.

It is useful to understand the causes and the impact on partners, how to prevent affairs, and how to heal after one has occurred. Today, with men and women working together and traveling away from home, there is a much greater opportunity to be unfaithful. Some of the reasons people have affairs include:

- Feeling emotionally disconnected, unappreciated, and lonely. The individual seeks others who can listen to their troubles and understand them;
- Feeling sexually dissatisfied, often in addition to the emotional disconnect;
- Being angry at our partner and wanting to "get even;" or
- Believing that monogamy may not be the perfect way to live.

Rarely are affairs just about sex. They usually occur because a partner feels a combination of the above factors.

Affairs may or may not lead to separation or divorce. If one has had an affair, all is not necessarily lost. Many couples work through the situation and, in time, they are able to regain trust and strengthen their marriage. After an affair is revealed, it is important to be honest with each other and take precautions, preventing a reoccurrence.

Sustaining Your Snuggle

When the turmoil has calmed down after one of you has been unfaithful, it is important to be there for each other's emotional needs, talking honestly and openly about your feelings and fears without blame.

If you are the person who was unfaithful, tell your partner what caused you to stray and explain what happened if they ask. Discuss what each of you can do to prevent future occurrences. Both partners need to be considered and respected, so work together to fulfill each other's needs.

Find ways to stay connected through conversation and activities. Plan a vacation for just the two of you to spend time together, reconnecting and making plans for the future that will assure you of better times ahead.

This Will Always Please Your Partner

The game of bridge requires an opening bid and a supporting response. If your partner opens with three hearts, you know they have a handful of hearts and they are asking you to join them with your hearts. You would like to respond "four hearts," but in bridge, like in love, you must play according to the cards you have been dealt.

The Road to Power Snuggling

With love, we have more opportunities than with bridge. Regardless of our partner's bid, with understanding and patience, we can almost always find ways to support them.

What is a bid from our love partner? A bid is anything they say or any action they take that elicits a response from us. "Good morning" is a bid. "I had a rough day today" is a bid. Questions such as "Would you like to go out to dinner?" or "Did you hear what happened downtown?" are also bids. A bid can be a smile, a frown, a touch on the shoulder.

We can respond positively, neutrally, or negatively to any bid. A simple bid such as "Good morning" can elicit these responses:

Positive: "It is a nice morning. Thanks for starting the coffee."
Neutral: "Uh-huh," as the responder continues to read the newspaper.
Negative: "Just like you, trying to make everything cheery on a dreary day."
Negative: Ignore the greeting, offering no response.

As in bridge, we need to determine the best way to connect with our partner's bids. Positive responses will bring love closer, and negative or neutral responses will push us further apart. This does not mean that if our partner lashes out at us, we have to counter with a positive response. But we should avoid upping the negative ante. We find that most bids offered each day allow for positive responses, even with couples who are having conflicts.

One of the quickest ways to overcome difficult times is by responding to our partner's bids with humor. People often say they love their partner for their sense of humor, and Howard Markman, a psychologist who works with couples in Colorado, notes, "When people are laughing together, they feel more positive toward each other. They're more likely to give each other the benefit of the doubt." (Polly Schulman, "Crack Me Up," PsychologyToday.com [July 1, 2006]). Markman's research shows that humor can quickly change our mood as long as it is used to join us together in a positive manner.

Sustaining Your Snuggle

A Swedish proverb says, "Shared joy is a double joy; shared sorrow is half a sorrow." Increase the joy in your relationship by connecting with your partner in positive ways. Look for humor in everyday situations, sharing jokes and relishing a good laugh together. Enjoy the upbeat mood, reminiscing about happy times in the past.

Add three positive responses to your partner's bids every day for the next two weeks. They will likely respond in kind. Together, you can create a number of relationship grand slams and share the joy.

A Powerful Way to Love

An old joke goes something like this: After her son is born, a mother calls the child "Bubbala," a Yiddish term of endearment. She calls, "Bubbala, would you like more oatmeal?", "Bubbala, it's time for your nap," and "Bubbala, that's a beautiful picture you drew."

Her son grows older and returns from his first day at school. His mother asks, "Bubbala, what did you learn in school today?" He replies, "I learned that my name is Irving!"

The Road to Power Snuggling

Obviously, Irving's mother got carried away with his nickname, but names hold special meaning for us. People love the sound of their names. When they hear their name, friends smile, strangers look up, and store personnel pay more attention. We even celebrate and immortalize adored names in song. In the musical *West Side Story,* Tony intones, "The most beautiful sound I ever heard:/Maria, Maria, Maria, Maria . . ./All the beautiful sounds of the world in a single word . . ./Maria, Maria, Maria, Maria . . . Maria!"

Nicknames are even more intimate. The monikers Honest Abe (Abraham Lincoln), Eminem (Marshall Bruce Mathers, III), and Lady Gaga (Stefani Joanne Angelina Germanotta) instantly identify the one special person with whom they are associated. We give our pets nicknames and say them with a special tone of voice. We lavish love on our children with nicknames. They feel comforted hearing their special name.

Sharing loving nicknames with our partner will have a similar effect. Using names, and pet names in particular, keeps our relationship tender. "Honey" and "Sweetie" are nice, but using a special nickname just for our partner helps to maintain a warm bond.

Sustaining Your Snuggle

If you have a unique name for your partner, use it more frequently.

If you have yet to choose one, it is never too late. Your partner will feel adored when they hear their special love name.

When Your Relationship Goes "Blah"

Ian is having a beer with Dave after work.

IAN: When I wake up in the morning, I say to Sarah, "Gooood Morning!" And what do you think she says?

DAVE: I don't know. What? Good morning?

IAN: No! That's the problem. She just says, "Uh-huh." Not even a big "Uh-huh." I can barely hear her. She's so sullen every day. I try to perk her up, but I can't. When we first met, she was upbeat and fun to be with.

DAVE: Well, I've seen her at parties. She's upbeat. She seems to be having a great time.

IAN: Sure, she's upbeat at parties. But with me, it's getting to be the same old, same old every week. We don't have fun together like we used to. After six years of marriage, things are definitely going downhill.

DAVE: That's how relationships are. They can't be exciting forever.

IAN: I thought ours would be different. I thought ours would keep getting better and better.

The Road to Power Snuggling

It is time for Ian and Sarah to get "remarried." If our relationship feels blah, we need to start fresh, renew our commitment, and begin a new marriage with our partner. To enjoy a lifetime of loving, we continually must make conscious and specific adjustments to keep our love alive. Every day, we should take a few minutes to think of ways to refresh our relationship. Our daily routine needs jump-starts to avoid boredom and indifference. Adjustments will also be required when we change jobs, have children, or move. Similarly, we need to adjust when there are changes in our finances or health.

All relationships will at times hit the same old, same old point. What was exciting when we first met tends to wind down and our commitment needs new energy. Successful couples "remarry" each other three or four times in a lifetime. Renewal requires effort and shifting to new attitudes, activities, travels, and adventures.

Sustaining Your Snuggle

Consciously tune in to your daily interactions with your partner. Notice nuances that signal indifference or boredom. What changes can you make together to restart your relationship? One person can take the lead, but both need to contribute ideas. Avoid placing the responsibility on your partner and thinking, "If my partner would only . . ." Your partner's role is not simply to make you happy.

To rekindle your romance, begin by finding the time to truly listen to each other's wishes, hopes, and dreams. Take action by pursuing these aspirations together. Plan one new activity together every month. You will gradually begin to renew your feelings of friendship and love in your long-term couplehood.

Counting the Ways He Doesn't Love Me

Hannah is talking to her sister, Sabrina:

HANNAH: And he gave me a birthday card, but all he wrote was, "Love, Gary." That's it. Is this the way to treat a spouse?
SABRINA: Nothing else?
HANNAH: Nothing, except some gooey words printed by the card company. I remember early on he'd bring me flowers. And you know that movie we all saw when the guy wrote a love poem on their fifth anniversary? Can't remember the name, but we saw it together. So why can't Gary say a little more than "love" with his name? And he hasn't directly told me "I love you" for years. In fact, I'm wondering if he really does love me. He certainly isn't as romantic as he was when we first met.
SABRINA: Yeah but I saw the way he looked at you lovingly during dinner the other night. And he had his arm around you walking home. Oh, and at the party, he bragged that you got a promotion at work. Hannah, the guy is trying. Give him a break.
HANNAH: He bragged about me?
SABRINA: Uh-huh. Looks like you're counting the ways he doesn't love you, instead of seeing the ways he does.

The Road to Power Snuggling

In her collection of love poems *Sonnets from the Portuguese,* Elizabeth Barrett Browning wrote, "How do I love thee? Let me count the ways" ("Sonnet 43"). Many years later, John Lennon referenced the immortal line when he wrote the song "Let Me Count the Ways":

Let me count the ways how I love you
It's like that gentle wind you feel at dawn
It's like that first sun that hits the dew
It's like that cloud with a gold lining telling us softly
That it'll be a good day, a good day for us
Thank you, thank you, thank you . . .

The ways we say "I love you" do not have to take the form of a love poem. Some of us are effusive; others much more subtle. Some bring gifts, while others do favors. Some are quite vocal about their love, yet others express themselves infrequently. Then there are those who are just there when we need them. Over time, the ways we express our love evolve and we show our affection very differently from when we first met.

To understand whether our partner loves us, we can focus on our daily life as a couple. There are countless ways people show their love. Some people bring their partner a cup of coffee every morning. Others care for the children, allowing their partner to sleep late. And still others may gently massage their partner's neck when muscles ache or simply listen when their partner has had a bad day. Connecting with special acts of kindness is a more powerful way to ensure the success of our long-term relationship than the love clichés portrayed in movies or gifts on special occasions.

Sustaining Your Snuggle

To find your way back to love, clear the air with your partner. Discuss and resolve issues that wear you down. Stop counting the ways you feel your partner fails to show their love. Focusing on their bothersome traits is a sure to way to ruin your relationship. Accept flaws when possible.

Look for ways your partner shows love and kind behaviors. Is it through a chore that they initiate or take over? Is it through something seemingly small, like passing you the dinner rolls without your asking? Or is it through a loving smile or touch? Regularly offer your own caring behaviors to your partner as well. Focus on building gratitude for what you have together.

We hear people say, "If they really love me, they would do these things automatically, to please me. Why should I have to ask?" Your partner is not a mind reader. Help them out by sharing your desires.

When Your Partner Needs Help

SETH: Well Sally's back from the hospital, so I have to figure out what comes next. The doctor said she'll be resting a lot for awhile. It's so odd seeing her lying there helpless. I wish I knew where to start. The kids keep asking when she's going to get up and play with them. They can't understand what's happened.

Then there's cooking meals, getting them off to school, and keeping the house up. We kept eating pizza when she was in the hospital. I have no idea when she'll be able to return to work. It's a nightmare!

GREGORY: Yeah, it's gotta be tough being in your shoes. There are so many uncertainties with this type of situation. We can help you out with food. I make a mean lasagna and Fiona is great with salads. We're here for you if you need anything, like looking after the kids. Give us a call, even if it's just to talk.

The Road to Power Snuggling

Many of us have experienced caring for a partner who is debilitated, even if temporarily. Difficult situations we may face as a couple include long-term unemployment, drug or alcohol dependency, depression, surgery, a major accident, or a life-threatening illness, to name just a few. During these times we worry whether we can survive. Questions pop into our mind: How are we going to pay the bills? Who will take care of the kids? Will our partner ever recover? What should I do next? It is challenging to keep life under control when our partner has issues requiring considerable attention. Family dynamics are disrupted and we might feel the problems will never end. However, we need to keep the situation in perspective without being overly optimistic or negative. Our behavior and attitude play an important part in our partner's comfort and recovery process.

We all have our quirks when we are down. Some people who are incapacitated prefer to be doted on with a cool compress, hugs, a massage, or soup in bed. Others find comfort in a quiet room and solitude, with no desire to communicate. Our partner's preferences may change depending on the severity and duration of the situation. We can make helpful suggestions; however, it is up to our partner to decide what will work for them during their recovery. We should let our partner know we understand what they are going through and help in ways that comfort them.

We can relieve some of our own stress by concerning ourselves with what needs to be done right now, rather than focusing on what may happen in the future. We may turn to the "Three A's" to help us get through the crisis: Appraise, Accept, and Adjust. First appraise the situation. We must understand what we are dealing with by researching literature and asking questions. Once we know the facts, we need to accept the situation. It is also useful to speak with friends who might be able to help. Then we can move on and provide necessary adjustments to help ourselves, our partner, and our family. Adjustments might include making changes at work or in our household and daily lifestyle. We also need to have an honest discussion with our partner on how the situation is impacting our lives, sharing our hopes and fears. Sexual desire may be hampered; however, there are many ways we can stay intimate, showing our partner they are still desired. At times when we feel overwhelmed, we need to take breaks to relax our mind and body. Having alone time is crucial and calming.

Sustaining Your Snuggle

We tend not to think about dire situations when life is copacetic. However, when a serious situation arises with your partner, stay well informed of the circumstances and discuss this information together. This is a time when your partner needs you most, both for physical and emotional support. When they want to talk, be there for them by listening, as their feelings and concerns are important in their recovery process.

While experiencing the upheaval, take special time to care for yourself. It is reassuring to know that even when you are down with little hope for change, people are resilient and healing will occur.

IX

What Is Love All About?

   The genius Albert Einstein had a number of love relationships, including two marriages. He was a romantic who wrote tender love letters. Yet if he were asked to explain what love is all about, he would likely have replied that understanding his general theory of relativity is child's play compared to understanding the complexities of love.

   We are born with an intense desire to love and be loved. Love is mysterious yet we know it when we have found it. Love lost can be more painful than physical pain. We constantly seek to understand what love is all about, and in that search, we may find opportunities to ensure the comfort, sustain the passion, and establish the lasting happiness that we all deserve.

Why Do We Love?

After graduating from college, Russell applied for the perfect public relations job with a great company. He had never wanted anything more. Competing against experienced applicants increased his desire to land the position. He spent most of his waking hours planning for the interview, fantasizing about what it would be like to work there, and hoping he would earn enough to buy his dream car. Lo and behold, he was selected.

Looking back, he realizes those wishes were trivial compared to the yearning he now has after falling in love with Lauren. Russell's love for Lauren is all-encompassing, leaving him both energized and frozen with fear. He is afraid he will say or do the wrong thing, and Lauren might reject him. In his office, he rereads the short email she sent when she accepted their first date. In his apartment, he keeps his phone close, afraid to pick it up and call her. He practices out loud what he will say when she answers, trying not to sound too excited.

After a few dates, he pictures Lauren's smile and the way her hair flows over her shoulders. He remembers the tone of her laugh as he curves his arm around her waist. Their conversations are etched into his memory. After a dinner date, he tries to recall whether she used the word "magnificent" or "wonderful" when referring to the restaurant, believing she was alluding to him. Surely, his love for Lauren is as important as being alive, for he could not imagine continuing the rest of his life without her.

The Road to Power Snuggling

Helen Fisher's book *Why We Love* describes how over hundreds of thousands of years people have needed to be loved and to offer love. This love is apart from the need for sexual union to continue the human race. Her research was conducted through a combination of interviews, questionnaires, and brain scans of people who recently had fallen in love. Dr. Fisher concluded that all individuals, regardless of their culture, whether they are straight or gay, or whether they are eighteen or eighty years old, seek a special person to love. An individual can only fall in love with one person at a time. When one falls in love, all other concerns take second place. She notes there is strong evidence that even animals such as elephants, foxes, and apes fall in love by carefully selecting and cherishing a particular mate. This indicates that evolution paved the way for wiring human brains to select a partner.

Though our genetics contribute to the process of falling in love, our experiences and decisions allow us to decide who we believe is most suitable to choose as a life partner. Our physiological need to beget children is much less important than our psychological need to love and to be loved. In 1943, Abraham Maslow published his classic paper, "A Theory of Human Motivation," in the *Psychological Review*. In his paper he describes how our physiological needs such as food, water, sleep, and sex are at the bottom of his pyramid of needs. Much farther up on the hierarchy is our need for love, friendship, and intimacy, indicating that love is not linked exclusively to genetics or evolutionary constraints. We seek someone to love who can meet our emotional needs and help us to expand what we believe are desirable character and ability traits. In this new, exciting relationship we have the opportunity to become more competent in areas to our liking. When we are attracted to each other and show kindness, we have the basic components for this growth.

Russell's romantic stage will fade within a few years, to be replaced with deep, long-term love. The romantic stage with all its neurological triggers helped Russell choose Lauren as his partner. Now, mutual support is required to enjoy long-term and fulfilling love. Like most couples, however, they will encounter Power Struggles along the way.

Sustaining Your Snuggle

As you grow in your love relationship by expanding your personality, also pay attention to the small things in your partnership that make you both happy. What gives each of you enjoyment? Is it reading the Sunday newspaper and sharing a big breakfast? Is it watching a movie together, pursuing a hobby you each enjoy, or just chilling out together?

Look for ways to laugh with each other and keep your relationship fresh and alive. Certainly, there are times when you set off negative emotions in the other. We have addressed ways to resolve such issues earlier in this book. However, once you are open to romantic behaviors, such as kind gestures and positive thoughts, new ideas will emerge. Your partner's response will please you.

The ABCs of Caring

BILLY: Wow, that's great, Renee. You brought home my favorite magazine. I really appreciate you thinking of me.
RENEE: You finally said it.
BILLY: Finally said what?
RENEE: You said you appreciate me. We've been together four years, and I rarely hear that you care about what I do for you.
BILLY: But you know I love you, don't you?
RENEE: Yeah, but when you specifically said you appreciate me, I felt a special glow. It's hard to describe, but I feel much closer to you right now.

The Road to Power Snuggling

It is not uncommon for couples to go for months without giving heartfelt appreciations. Sure, we may hear a thanks for taking out the trash or for running an errand. We all know how to say thank you. However, showing our partner gratitude for who they are and what they do is more challenging and more important. When they hear our meaningful and enthusiastic words of appreciation, it excites their emotions, bringing them much closer to us.

Appreciation directly impacts our brain. Relationship educator Athena Staik, Ph.D., explains that it should be no surprise that positive actions generate positive brain reactions. She notes that gratitude releases oxytocin, one of the chemicals our body produces during sexual intimacy, into the bloodstream, which floods our body with feelings of love, safety, and connection.

Gratitude and expressions of appreciation are learned behaviors. Over the years, we have asked couples we counsel to tell us what their parents admired about them. Sadly many, if not most, could not think of one compliment they received from their parents. If we never heard specific words of appreciation while growing up, we never learned the importance of appreciating others. As we begin to offer our partner thanks, it may seem awkward. However, it becomes more natural as we get in touch with our feelings of gratitude and we experience the results.

With the ABCs of caring as our guide, we can appreciate our partner for their:

Appearance: Their smile, their hair, their clothes.
Behavior: How they have helped us, what they have given us, how they hugged us, or how they supported our children or relatives.
Character: Their empathy, their sensitivity, their athletic ability, their artistic ability, their special intelligence, or their musical talents.

A "Thanks for bringing in the mail" or "You look pretty today" will bring us closer. To add more tenderness, we suggest these steps:

1. Look into your partner's eyes. You might want to hold hands.
2. Say, "I appreciate you for . . ."
3. Deepen your appreciation by adding, "And that's special to me because . . ."
4. It is also helpful if the person receiving the appreciation repeats back, "So you appreciate me for . . . and that's special to you because. . . ." The one offering the appreciation will know they have been heard.

We should use this exercise daily or at least weekly. When we practice one or more of the ABCs, our love is sure to grow. Though most of us know our partner loves us, we all require a daily refueling of approval to keep the fire burning in our heart.

Sustaining Your Snuggle

When is the last time either of you gave your partner a genuine compliment? You know what you appreciate in each other. You know the attributes you admire. Share what is on your mind. When you conceal these thoughts, your partner is deprived of your true feelings.

Your partner will delight in your kind words, even if they react modestly. Offer new appreciations each day instead of repeating the same ones. "I liked dinner tonight" loses its appeal when uttered the same way every night. Beware of using appreciations that are wrapped in frustrations such as, "I appreciate that you finally emptied the dishwasher." Be creative with your choices and speak from your heart.

We Are All Born to Love

Just before bedtime, Zach, a three year old, looks at his six-month-old sister, Josie. He picks up his favorite stuffed Teddy bear and places it next to Josie in her crib. He croons, "Here little Josie. You sleep good now. You sleep good now."

The Road to Power Snuggling

Many mammals are empathic. Just as we are born with tongue receptors to distinguish sweetness and saltiness, we also are born with the ability to empathize and a desire to be kind. A 1950s experiment with rats trained to press a lever for food found these rats less likely to press the lever when they realized that other rats in a nearby cage received an electric shock at the same time. In another experiment at Yale University, babies were shown several photographs of a person struggling to climb a hill, with a second person trying to help and a third person trying to hinder. The babies, as young as six months, indicated preference for the helper over the hinderer. Mammals as diverse as chimpanzees and elephants can empathize and understand what is kind and what is unkind. They are born with a desire to either support or appropriately punish these behaviors. Their brain understands what is fair or unfair.

We are also born to understand what love feels like. Throughout life, we tap into our natural ability to love. From the time we are infants, we have the ability to connect with a smile or a touch. At just a month or two we flirt with our parents with coos and facial expressions, waiting for their response. We crave attachment and learn to trust. As we become adults, we continue to seek love. Without planning, we naturally express adoration for our partner with gestures, smiles, eye glances, touching, and kind words. We yearn for closeness and our partner mirrors our behavior, accepting our overtures.

We hunger for that love and hope it will last forever. As Dr. Sue Johnson explains, the concern underlying many of our relationship questions and fears is that we are not loved by our partner. "Distressed partners may use different words but they are always asking the same basic questions, 'Are you there for me? Do I matter to you? Will you come when I need you, when I call?'" (*Hold Me Tight* [New York: Little, Brown and Company, 2008], 46-47).

Sustaining Your Snuggle

Focus on your own behavior. Imagine that you are a stranger looking at yourself and your partner trying to understand what is occurring. Are you reaching out by using the empathic skills you inherited at birth?

When your relationship is strained, look beyond your partner's anger and realize that they are hurting inside. We all have a little boy or little girl hidden in us that sometimes feels hurt and needs to be consoled. At times like this, it is especially important to be there for each other, to soothe emotional needs.

The Gift of Wishes

Tyler is ten years old, and he's speaking with Aunt Hannah.

TYLER: I'm scared I won't pass the math test tomorrow.
AUNT HANNAH: No?
TYLER: No, it's too hard. I wish I could talk to my mom.
AUNT HANNAH: What would you say to her if she were here?
TYLER: I'd tell her I'm good at adding and subtracting but multiplication is very, very hard.
AUNT HANNAH: What do you think she'd say?
TYLER: She'd probably say that I learned other things, and I probably could learn multiplication. And it's okay if I get some problems wrong because everyone does.
AUNT HANNAH: What else would you say to her?
TYLER: I'd tell her that I wish I could go to the park with her, and we could paddle a canoe in the lake and laugh and splash water on each other.
AUNT HANNAH: That sounds like a lot of fun.
TYLER: Yeah. I think I'll go study for the math test now.

Tyler's mom died in a car accident two years earlier. Now he lives with Aunt Hannah, who knows that acknowledging Tyler's wishes is important.

The Road to Power Snuggling

Whether we are speaking with a child, our partner, or a neighbor, sharing our wishes and dreams is a gift that brings us closer. Our partner might say, "It would be great to take a vacation to Paris." Our first inclination might be, "You know that's impossible given our finances. Besides, who would care for the kids?" We may fear that if we validate our partner's wish, we have to act on it. Validation does not mean we agree. It simply means we acknowledge the other's feelings. We can provide understanding by saying, "I can see why you'd love to go to Paris. We'd eat in a café, walk along the Champs Elysees, and you could speak the French you've learned."

Some wishes are pie-in-the-sky with little chance of coming to fruition; other wishes are granted. We all have desires for something that will enhance our life or help someone we love. Regardless of whether our wishes come true, these innermost thoughts are worthy of sharing. When our partner grasps how these wishes excite our senses, both our hearts feel joyful.

Sustaining Your Snuggle

You have an opportunity to warm your relationship whenever your partner expresses their wishes. If you hear, "I wish it would finally rain so I won't have to keep watering the garden," you can respond, "Raindrops would be nice to hear, and the plants would love it." This supports your partner, regardless of the weather forecast.

Offering the gift of wishes costs nothing. You are not agreeing. You are not making commitments. You are simply showing your partner that you love them and support their desires and dreams.

Creating Loving Cells

Ralph wasn't a poet, but Sheila found the following note on the kitchen table after he had left for work:

> About what you told me last night,
> I'm sorry I failed to listen, I lost sight.
> You were right, I shouldn't pout;
> Tonight we'll dance and we'll eat out!
>   Love and hugs, Ralph

Before she left for work, Sheila texted Ralph:

> Ralph, you are such a dear;
> Your note to me brought joyful tears.
> A love like yours is an amazing winner!
> Yes, I'll join you for a delicious dinner. ☺
>   Much love, Sheila

All day Ralph and Sheila felt great about their exchange, and they laughed as they recalled the notes while dining that evening. What neither of them realized was that they had physically changed their brain cells by adding thousands of "love" neurons during their exchange of notes and their anticipation of their reunion throughout the day.

The Road to Power Snuggling

When we exercise, major physiological changes occur in our body. We jog in the park and see beautiful trees; we hear chirping and we smell spring enveloping us. Jogging releases endorphins in our head, and our muscles carry us forward as if they are on automatic pilot. We have learned that regular exercise strengthens our bones, improves our heart efficiency, and promotes the growth of our muscles in the areas where we put the most effort.

In addition, recent brain scanning research proves that when we change our method of thinking to a more loving way, physical changes occur in our brains. We add love neuron cells to the 100 billion cells in our brain. Dr. Helen Fischer, a biological anthropologist, and Dr. Lucy Brown, a neuroscientist, have scanned the brains of an estimated one hundred people in love and found that their brain neurons change after they fall in love, driving them to want to be with their partner.

For decades, scientists believed that our brains changed little after adulthood. However, new scanning technology shows that our brain changes dramatically with behavior changes, in the same way muscles grow. In each case, blood is pumped into the areas most used. Loving behaviors add neurons to our brain's amygdala area, creating a feeling of well-being.

What do these experiments mean for Ralph and Sheila, as well as for all of us? If we increase our positive behavior, we are constructing a physical change in the amygdala area of our brain by expanding our love neurons. With these additional neurons, caring behaviors become easier and more automatic, just as increased muscle from exercising reduces our effort in lifting heavy objects.

Sustaining Your Snuggle

After a spat with your partner, the last thing you may want to do is write them a love poem as Ralph did. But whoever begins the process of reconciling has the power to change the relationship. It takes strength of character to be the first. Changes won't occur if no one initiates them.

Offer your partner daily caring behaviors. You will be creating tens of thousands of love neurons.

The Missing Cups of Tea and Thee

Yoko Ono wrote an article for the *New York Times* on December 8, 2010, thirty years after her husband, John Lennon, was murdered. In the article she recalls a chat they had in the middle of the night in the kitchen of their New York City apartment.

It seems John made their tea by putting the tea in the pot then adding the hot water. But he had recently spoken with his Aunt Mimi, and she told him he was supposed to pour the hot water in first then add the tea. He was sure she had taught him to put the tea in first. Yoko notes that when they realized they had been brewing tea the wrong way all these years, they broke into laughter. Yoko and John kept their love alive by laughing and enjoying the little things together. Yoko writes, "That was in 1980. Neither of us knew it was to be the last year of our life together."

John Lennon was a musician, a singer, and a songwriter. He rose to worldwide fame as a founder of the Beatles, the most commercially successful band in the history of popular music. He was murdered on December 10, 1980. He was forty years old. What a shock and a loss to Yoko and to the world!

The Road to Power Snuggling

In our daily life we are bombarded with petty issues that we cannot avoid. We become furious if someone cuts us off when we spot a parking space; we are upset for hours when we are unfairly billed by our credit card company; and we get angry at our partner when they forget to pick up donuts at the store. When someone we know dies, it is not unusual to view our life in a different perspective. We realize that time is precious and we need to appreciate what is really important and recognize what is not important. Certainly we have to deal with everyday annoyances and other issues that are broader in scope. However, this does not mean we cannot find time to periodically make adjustments as we reassess our values and the way we relate to our partner. In doing so, we are likely to rediscover their attributes, bringing us closer.

Sustaining Your Snuggle

We tend not to think about what our life would be like if we lost our partner although we know there is no guarantee that we will always be together. Take the time to recognize the things you love about your partner and communicate what you mean to each other.

- What would you miss most if your partner were not with you? Tell them now.
- What memories would you cherish? Share them now.
- What words of love have you been meaning to speak but have been holding back? Speak them now.
- What do you wish you had done together and have not? Do what is possible.

Appreciating what your partner has to offer will bring you joy every day.

Our Upside-Down View of Love

SEEKER: What I really want is a partner who will love me, respect me, and enjoy being with me. I want someone with whom I can feel comfortable being myself. When we first met, that was how it was. We had unbelievable love!

LOVE ADVISOR: And what happened?

SEEKER: I tried to be a loving partner. I kept up my appearance, I worked hard to earn a living, I helped the needy, and I felt I was interesting. But over the years things changed. We lost the experience of being in love. Now we have so many conflicts. I miss the old days.

LOVE ADVISOR: So are you still working hard to make your partner love you?

SEEKER: Yes, but it doesn't work.

LOVE ADVISOR: Your goal is upside-down. Your first goal should be to learn how to love. Only then will your other efforts succeed.

SEEKER: But I am told by friends and by messages in movies and in articles all the things I should do to be loved. The TV and the Internet are flooded with ideas: look great, be accomplished, and be kind to one's partner.

LOVE ADVISOR: I'm afraid those sources have it upside-down too. Think of the people who loved you when you were young and those whom you love unconditionally now. You don't love your children, friends, or even your pets because they are pretty or accomplished. You love them because you learned how to love. You see their wonderful parts and accept the parts that aren't so wonderful.

On a lesser scale, you might love dancing, a sunrise through the fog, a sumptuous meal, sports, yoga, or discussion groups. Why? Because you have worked to understand the subtleties of these experiences. You have learned the art of loving.

SEEKER: I don't understand. How will this help my partner and me regain our love?

LOVE ADVISOR: It sounds like you spend much time trying to please your partner. Instead of trying to be loved, focus on being loving. Admire what is happening in the world around you. You will feel love by seeing perfection in an imperfect friend, by hearing the melodic voice of a singer, by relishing a conversation with a young child, or by reading a fascinating book. This in turn will allow you and your partner to feel greater love flowing between you.

The Road to Power Snuggling

In 1956, psychologist Erich Fromm wrote *The Art of Loving*. Fromm says that love in Western societies is about acquiring a love object and desiring the highest quality in appearance, success, and personality to match our attributes. This practice leads to failure because the initial romantic infatuation invoked by these traits naturally diminishes with all couples over time. If we see love as an emotional experience and a matter of accomplishment, we will never find true, long-lasting love. Fromm says we only achieve lasting love by mastering the art of loving. He wrote, "Is love an art? Then it requires knowledge and effort. Or is love a pleasant sensation, which to experience is a matter of chance, something one 'falls into' if one is lucky? . . . Most people see the problem of love as that of being loved, rather than of loving. Hence the problem to them is . . . how to be loveable" ([New York: Harper Perennial, 2006], 1). Fromm's philosophy is as true now as it was more than fifty years ago, and his book is still being published and read in more than thirty languages.

Through concentration, discipline, and patience, we learn the beauty of observing love all around us. More importantly, we can cast a positive light on our partner as we focus on their inner beauty while accepting their imperfections. We can appreciate our differences and benefit by sharing ideas. Though we all see the beauty of the world through our own eyes, sharing our thoughts with our partner will enable them to become enlightened and to better understand what is in our mind and in our heart.

Sustaining Your Snuggle

Think of someone you greatly admire. Chances are that person is selfless and truly listens to others. They appreciate day-to-day life without the expectation of anything in return. They are fascinated with the world, which guides their growth.

Following that example, notice the beauty around you and take in the warm sensations. Set your goal to expand your capacity to love. Allow your gratitude to flow into your relationship, accepting your partner without judgment. Focus on your partner's attributes and overlook their imperfections.

As you practice the art of loving, you are less likely to be drawn into daily spats. Your partner will feel a more loving environment, and tensions will diminish. Your differences will no longer be a source of conflict but will instead become something you respect and admire. Through this journey, you will rediscover the beauty of the relationship you had when you first met but on a much deeper level.

X

Rachel in Love

Love relationships evolve through various stages over months and years. After falling in love, couples will enjoy a great many wondrous times. They will also endure a number of conflicts. Your relationship's success will be determined by each partner's willingness to try on some new ideas and incorporate them into daily life. We believe most couples can find ways to overcome their major disagreements and enjoy the bliss of love. With determination and acceptance of each other's differing values and ideas, your love will continue to grow. You will then be able to enjoy the romantic connection that couples have sought ever since man and woman walked on Earth.

This book began at the start of Rachel and Bradley's love affair. How did their relationship unfold? Their experiences together, revealed through the following excerpts from their journals, help us understand the evolution of relationships. The journals include both their Power Struggles and their Power Snuggles. By focusing on their thoughts and feelings and by learning from their interactions, we hope you will better understand how to strengthen your own relationship.

The Journals of Rachel and Bradley

Rachel

March 10: Sunday morning I was jogging in the park, and out of nowhere a dog came bounding at me, jumping up with his tail wagging, begging to be petted. I was frightened until I saw his owner shouting, "Down, Plato!" It turns out this guy, Bradley, is so cute that I quickly forgot about Plato and his muddy paws. I don't remember how many times Bradley apologized, but he was clearly embarrassed. Then as we chatted he stroked Plato's fur, explaining how his dog was usually very well behaved. The poor thing looked up at me like he was smiling and asking for forgiveness. Before I knew it Bradley suggested we grab coffee at that outdoor café on Maple Street.

Bradley's really with it. He works with information technology and knows all about the universe since he minored in astronomy, and he's well educated on Russian novelists and—really cool for a guy—it sounds like he cooks gourmet. Dad can't even boil water.

Only problem: he seemed kind of shy when he asked for my cell number. Maybe he asked because guys are supposed to. So I don't know if I'll hear from him.

Bradley

March 12: I met this girl in the park a few days ago. Rachel. Very pretty and interested in what I had to say. And she has this confident way about her. She's so different from Sheila. Rachel knows zilch about recipes and probably lives on take-out food. But she's big on botany and knows loads about plants, flowers, and stuff.

It bugs me that I want to text her and ask her out. But I still want to keep dating Sheila, not that we're serious or anything. Guess there's nothing wrong with asking Rachel to meet and do some park talk. Truth is, I've been there the last couple of days hoping I'd bump into her. She has this great smile and a cool way about her. Can't explain on paper.

Rachel

March 13: Bradley hasn't texted or called me, so forget him. Can't win 'em all.

It rained continuously today. I couldn't get out to visit clients' gardens; it sucks that landscaping work is so dependent on weather. And it's Friday the Thirteenth. Ugh! Looks like a lonely weekend too.

Bradley

March 18: Confession: I texted Rachel. She answered a few hours later. She can't meet me tomorrow. Said she's jogging day after tomorrow if that works for me. Asked if I'd bring Plato. Not sure if she's interested in me. Seems like she's more into Plato. Whatever.

Rachel

March 20: I met Bradley again after he texted. Wow! I don't have time to write the whole connection. Let's just say we did more talking than jogging, although he has a nice loping way of jogging, like he's flying three feet above the track. Maybe it's me who's flying high! ☺

He has this cute way of talking that makes me want to hug him. He's kind of shy and not at all pretentious. His name, "Bradley," keeps popping into my mind. I love the way it looks on paper: *Bradley*, Bradley, *Bradley*, **bradley**, B r a d l e y, ℬradley . . .

Bradley

March 22: I saw that R girl again. Even dreamt about her. In the dream she was talking with all this pep. Couldn't make out the words so I kept asking, "What? What are you saying?" She was smiling at me like we were doing something special. In real life, I don't remember what we talked about, but the rhythm was powerful—like a super nova exploding.

Rachel

March 26: It's been days, and I expected Bradley to call but he didn't. So I took a big risk, called him, and asked if he wanted to join me at Kathy and Dan's party. I never call guys I've just met. Anyone who knows me knows that's not my style. Also I'm a little uncomfortable going to Kathy and Dan's. Since they got married they've had fights so you never know when they might explode.

Anyway Bradley said, "Sure, what's the address? What time should I be there?" That's it. For a second I thought the line went dead. I didn't know what to say after that so I just gave him the time and address. I hope he shows up. Sort of reminds me of Dad when he talks staccato-like. You have to be a mind reader to know what Dad's thinking. I'll know whether Bradley's dependable if he makes it to Kathy's. If he doesn't, screw him.

Rachel

March 28: Bradley finally got to the party 46 minutes late. Can you imagine that: 46 minutes late! I bit my tongue and acted like it was no big deal. I asked if the traffic was bad, and all he said was no, like "Why'd you ask?" After I unwound from waiting we had a great time. When we walked into Kathy and Dan's backyard, Bradley asked me to identify some plants. He seemed impressed when I rattled off common and Latin names.

B continues to fascinate. He talked about how astronomers are virtually positive that the Earth isn't just a fluke but one of many Earthlike planets. Whoa! We're only a speck! That made me feel stupid stressing about him being 46 Earth-minutes late.

Rachel

April 4: B texted me a few days ago, "U want to go eat at the place on Maple St. Fri. nite?" Of course I waited a few hours to reply. Then waited a few hours more. Finally texted back at 11:30 p.m. and said, "OK, what time?" His text came back in 23 seconds: "7. Meet there, ok?"

We met and talked up a storm. He's so easy to talk with, looking straight into my eyes and taking it all in. Must confess I talked more, but he had lots to say too. Told me he has an older brother, George, and younger sister, Felicia, who happens to be the same age as Missy, so we both grew up with little sisters. His dad owns a produce market, but while they were growing up, a supermarket opened on the same block, competing with the business, so they didn't have much money.

Bradley

April 4: Flyin' to the moon with this Rachel girl. R has a younger sister same age as Felicia. She told me her old man doesn't talk lots but knows computers inside and out like I do.

Felt bad when Shelia called me and I had to tell her I've been very busy at work so can't see her much. She even offered to walk Plato while I'm at work, but I told her Jim next door works at home and takes Plato out. Hope she doesn't see R and me together.

Rachel

May 1: Can you believe it's been two months since I met Bradley! Well, almost two months. We've seen each other every Saturday and most Sundays. We keep talking and not worrying about what to say. I've never felt so comfortable with anyone before. Of course I can't tell him everything about me. That'd be dangerous, not that I have anything remarkable to hide.

But sometimes I worry, not only because of Kathy and Dan and their problems, but I remember Mom screaming at Dad for being late or "not thinking straight," whatever that meant. Also, I never saw Dad put his arm around Mom. He'd just come home, give her a quick kiss, then head for the computer. Absolutely no affection.

It was scary when Mom screamed. She has this high-pitched voice and I worried the neighbors would hear. I remember taking my sisters, Erin and Missy, into the bedroom and closing the door. I'd take out a board game, trying to pretend nothing was wrong. When the house became quiet, we'd ease the door open. Then we'd eat around the table and Dad would crack a joke as if nothing had happened. But Mom would have tight lips and a frozen face. After that it was hard to swallow my food.

I know if Bradley and I stay together I'll never scream like Mom. No way.

Bradley

May 3: We went to a movie, Rachel's choice, about a multi-generational family. There was lots of arguing and a huge cast of characters and personalities. Exhausting to watch but glad we saw it.

Rachel and I had a huge fight afterwards. Maybe I should've kept my mouth shut, but it ticked me off to see how she wastes money. She dropped me off to buy tickets. Instead of parking on the street one block away she paid $8 for the parking lot. She said she always pays for convenience and it's worth it. I couldn't believe it. Eight bucks so she wouldn't have to walk one block! What if we ever decide to get married? We'd go broke spending like that.

While she drove me back to my apartment, she yelled at me for being upset with her. I clammed up. Can't take that noise. It's extreme and I'm outta there when it happens.

When we got to my place, we talked in the car for almost an hour. Good thing, since it cleared the air some. Seems her dad, who made tons of dough, would pay for parking too—even valet service. His motto: It doesn't pay to go second class. Yeah, fine. But I had to work my way through college and cook most meals on a one-burner stove in the dorm. Told Rachel I thought $8 was pricey. When she drove off we still didn't agree but we weren't as upset. I can see this kind of thing happening again. Wonder if all couples argue over that stuff.

Rachel

May 3: Bradley and I had a fight on Saturday. We saw this great film about a large family who were always arguing to try to resolve their problems. Then we had our own argument. Can you believe this? Bradley was upset because I paid a few dollars to park the car. The movie was about to start and the street parking was a few blocks away so I pulled into a lot. If he's going to be so cheap, what'll happen if we ever get married? We'd be on a super-tight budget if it's all about him. Ugh!

But I was careful not to yell at him. Just raised my voice a little when I told him I felt bad he was so upset over such a trivial matter. At least we were able to talk about it afterwards. Seems his family almost went broke when the big supermarket opened near his dad's produce market, so he's worried about spending pennies. Maybe as we both make more, he'll calm down about parking.

Rachel

May 4: I called B before he left for work and told him I was sorry that we had the disagreement. Not that I was at fault or sorry for paying for parking—after all it was my money—but sorry he felt I yelled at him. Next time I'll work on being calmer. He said he understood and he knew we'll keep having discussions to soften things when times get tough. He has such a nice way with words.

Rachel

May 9: Today Bradley and I drove to one of those little towns where they have artsy shops. It was a glorious spring day with maple and oak trees heavy with swollen buds. The town had fresh tulips beds the color of the bright crayons I had as a kid. We wandered around stores looking at umpteen kitschy things *not* to buy.

Then we found a small bookstore. My eye caught a copy of *Our Town*. I remembered when I was Emily in my senior play. I suggested we buy it and read it together. Bradley insisted on paying. I guess he's generous when it comes to books. (I've got to stop thinking about the parking ordeal!) We found a bench in a small churchyard and took turns reading. It was such a pretty setting with tulips glowing and acorns on the ground left over from the fall. I read the Stage Manager's part and the female parts. Bradley read the other lines. I was taken when his eyes started to tear up as George visits Emily's grave after she dies in childbirth. We read the whole play in one sitting. By then it was dusk. The street lights blinked on so we could make out the last few pages.

As Bradley drove us back he reached for my hand now and then, twisting his thumb around mine. I felt like a kitten purring all the way home.

Rachel
May 10: We did it. Bradley stayed over for the first time. Need I say more? It was incredible!

In the morning we made breakfast. He searched my fridge and threw together this yummy mushroom and tomato omelet. Maybe I'll try it sometime. I've never made omelets so it was a treat. But I did make the toast and coffee.

Bradley
May 10: Stayed over at Rachel's last night. Man, she's unbelievably awesome. Can't stop thinking about it!

Rachel
June 15: It's gardening season, so I'm working my butt off with little time to write. All my friends know Bradley and I are an item. Usually he stays at my place on weekends, but a few times I've stayed at his digs. Wish I could get his place organized. Books on the floor, sofa pillows everywhere: what a mess. The dirty dishes in the sink drive me batty.

Bradley
June 30: Rae is great. Things are flowing like the rings around Saturn.

We have disagreements but seem to find a way of talking it over and figuring it out. She has this way of complaining but not complaining. She said she got worried last Sunday when I told her I'd be at her place at 3:00 and I wasn't there 'til 4:00. She meant when I shot the hoops with my buddy Dave and the gang. I had forgotten the time. She wants me to text if I'm going to be late. "Sure," I said. "Next time I'll call. Don't want to worry you." It'll be a big deal remembering to text her. But I'll give it a go since she's obviously upset about it.

I did call her this week after the game went to overtime. She was surprised and thanked me. Seems her Dad is forever late so she's very touchy about times, down to the nanosecond.

Rachel
July 1: Bradley just doesn't listen to me. He calls from my place asking when I'll be home so he can start dinner. I told him earlier I had to meet a client and I'd be home late so we couldn't see each other tonight. I tell him something important and his mind is floating in outer space. I couldn't hold it in. I let him know I can't take feeling invisible. I need him to listen.

Bradley
July 1: We had a little screw-up today. Rachel blew up at me for "not listening." I came to her place after she claims she told me she'd be working late. She talks all the time; I can't get a word in edgewise, lengthwise, or whatever. When we first met, I loved her enthusiasm but now it feels too, too much. I could never listen to every tiny, little, wee atom of a word she spits out. Who could?

Rachel
July 2: Bradley was annoyed at me for being angry at him. He didn't answer his phone all day. No way am I going to call until he calls me!

Bradley
July 2: I can't keep seeing someone who gets so upset and jabbers away so much. Stayed away from her all day. Don't know if I'll even answer the phone tomorrow. Probably not.

Rachel
July 3: I didn't call him today, just worked extra hard in the office. I picked

up my cell phone many times to text but changed my mind. I can't knuckle under. He'll have to call first. Tonight I'll do the park, jog, and unwind.

Bradley
July 3: Rae still hasn't called. Tonight I'll get in some jogging and forget the whole stupid thing. What do I care? I couldn't care less. Before I met her things were OK. I was just fine. Really.

Rachel
July 3, evening: So I got to the park and started my jog. One lap around and I heard barking. And who was chasing me? Plato, of course! He ran towards me and it was all I could do to keep his muddy paws off. Right behind comes Bradley with a sheepish grin. He opened his arms to hug me and I couldn't resist. He held me tight while other joggers flew past. I started to cry and his eyes watered. He kept stroking my back. We had dinner on Maple Street and kept gazing at each other, holding hands under the table.

Tomorrow is July 4, so we're off from work and going to see fireworks with Bradley's friend Dave and his new girlfriend, Carla. Hope there aren't fireworks between any of us. I can't deal with any more fighting.

Rachel
July 12: Things are back to normal. Saturday we went hiking with Kathy and Dan near a lake about two hours from town. Dan kept teasing Kathy for not climbing the mountain fast enough even though Bradley and I were staying behind to help her up. It makes me appreciate how kind Bradley is.

Bradley
August 1: Well, I screwed up royally at work. What a holy disaster. I told Rae when I got to her place. In fact I talked a lot about it. She just listened, nodded, and said she understood. How was I to know this client wanted a special program installed? I just gave them the basic one. No one told me differently.

After a while she said, "Yeah, every job has sticking points." She said that anybody would have felt awful about it if they went through what I did. She told me she once put koi fish in a client's pond with loads of lilies and the koi ate the lilies in two days. As we ate dinner she listened to my woes again. I felt better and slept OK.

Rachel

August 15: I haven't seen my folks for months, so last week I said I'd drive up. It's a 2¾ hour drive. I asked Bradley to come along. He seemed surprised, but I told him I hate driving a long way alone and he knows they've heard about him. He agreed to come and even offered to drive.

My folks really like him, especially Dad. Mom was her curious self, which is putting it nicely. She asked Bradley a gazillion questions about work, his parents, how many siblings he has and what they do, where he went to school, and on and on. I tried to stop her but it's like trying to halt invasive bamboo. Bradley answered her directly but didn't say much about his dad's produce market.

Then Erin and Missy stopped over, so Bradley met the whole family. My sisters made a big fuss over him. They laughed a bunch and Erin gave Bradley the head's up on me going nuts when it comes to being on time.

Bradley

August 16: Met Rae's family. It was kind of stressful. I felt like I was this new product being inspected by *Consumer Reports*. Her dad was great. He knows a fair amount about computer operating systems. He also knows I'm into astronomy and asked why Pluto is no longer considered a planet.

Don't know if I passed her mom's quality control test though. She was friendly and said she was "so happy" I was able to drive up with Rachel. Even though she had heard a lot about me she peppered me with tons of questions, except she didn't seem at all interested in the produce market.

Rae's sisters were very friendly, especially Missy. They like much of the same music as me and we got into favorite movies.

As we drove home I breathed easier, flicked the radio on, and caught up on baseball scores. Rae rested her head on my shoulder, sometimes dozing off. Felt fabulous.

Rachel

August 24: So after we saw my family, Bradley said I should meet his. They're three hours away in a different direction. It was a super visit! I was nervous when we arrived and had a headache but soon felt better. His parents are gems! Really sweet. His dad cracks jokes and it was fun seeing how they all hugged. Very touchy-feely. I met his brother and his younger sister. Felicia is Missy's age but very different. Felicia is quieter. She plays the flute in her college orchestra.

I even saw the produce market. It's much larger than I imagined with a great spread of every fresh fruit and vegetable, including organic. His dad told me they added these items to get a competitive edge over the supermarket. They also have beers, sodas, breads, jams, and nuts.

Bradley

August 24: Rae came home with me. The folks whispered that they really like her. George and Felicia stopped by and he behaved himself mostly but told Rachel to keep "that madman" away from the computer and the night skies. Of course Rae seemed right at home with everyone, making sure she talked to each of them. She even asked Felicia about her flute playing and George about his tennis game.

Rachel

September 8: Bradley got a promotion last week. I'm so proud of him! He's getting two new IT accounts and I think his salary went up considerably, but he was mum about the amount. Said he was the only one in his group promoted. To celebrate I'm getting him that book he wants about solar eclipses.

Bradley

October 1: Rachel took me to this mansion and showed me the amazing garden she planned. The owner, a woman who must be into her eighties, told me over and over how she's thrilled with Rae's design. It even has a pond with a waterfall, lily pads, and fish—no koi. I'm sure when we're married we'll have a big garden. We'll grow herbs and sunflowers for my special dishes. Oh yeah, my promotion came through! I'm ridin' high!

Rachel

November 10: This weekend with B was amazing. All I said was "My bedroom needs painting. It's looking shabby. I'll hire a painter." And he said "No way! You and I can paint it ourselves and save mucho bucks. We'll do it in a few hours." (Yeah, right!)

Next day I selected this light bluish-green color and pearl for the trim after searching through two million colors all called white. We ended up painting the entire weekend! Neither of us are pros, but we had lots of fun and it turned out great.

Bradley hugged and kissed me after finishing each wall, so things got carried away for awhile. Wouldn't mind tackling another room next weekend. ☺

Rachel

November 15: While jogging this evening I noticed my shirt was inside-out. I was embarrassed but Bradley didn't care. It got me thinking about awkward moments. So I asked him if he's ever been embarrassed. He told me when he was fifteen, he was a strong swimmer and was at the beach. He heard this girl in the water screaming for help. She was waving frantically toward the shore. Quick as a gold medalist, he dove into the water, swam to her, grabbed her (like in the Red Cross lifesaving course), and began pulling her to shore. Then she shouted, "What are you doing?" He said, "You shouted, 'Help!'" She said, "No I didn't! I was shouting 'Helen' to my friend!" (OMG!)

Of course he then asked me to tell him if I was ever embarrassed. I mentioned the time I was in seventh grade and brought my friend Zina home. When we opened the door my parents were in a screaming match, using words that shouldn't have reached our ears. They didn't hear us come in, so I had to talk loudly to Zina before they realized we were home and stopped. I could've died.

After we told our stories we hugged. I think true love is when you're OK telling each other everything, even when you are embarrassed. It's great that Bradley was open enough to tell me the Helen story. I feel he trusts me.

Bradley

December 18: I took Rae to my office holiday party with the usual good food and booze. It's so cool how she fits in with any group. Within minutes she's chatting with my coworkers and boss as though they're already good friends. She gets right into their interests, asking them questions.

I usually loathe those parties and end up in a corner, nursing a drink. But with Rae there, looking and sounding beautiful, I talked up a storm. I even told them the joke about the rabbit in North Carolina. They exploded! The staff kept asking, "What drugs are you on?" After, I told Rachel how proud I was of her and she shrugged. Sometimes she has trouble accepting praise.

Bradley

January 20: Rae keeps surprising me. Since it's indoor planning season she can leave work early. So I go to her place as usual to make dinner but—surprise—she got hold of a cookbook and roasted a whole chicken with orange sauce. So good! She also made wild rice, spinach salad, and even baked corn muffins. She apologized since the muffins were kind of dark. She said they were "burnt," but I still ate them. Before this meal her specialty was French toast on Sunday mornings.

Bradley
January 31: Ran into Sheila in town. I haven't seen her for months. I'd hoped to avoid her, but she saw me from afar, walked right up, and said, "I hear through the grapevine you're seeing someone. Best of luck." I felt very uneasy. I said, "Yep, just dating" to let her know right off I'm not getting married or anything. I asked her the usual stuff: how was her job and how was her brother getting along in the army. She could tell I wasn't really interested and gave me the "Everything's fine" response. She mentioned she was rereading Dostoyevsky's *Crime and Punishment* and I didn't know what to say except, "Good book. Bye!" Maybe it was her way of showing we were close once. It felt so awkward. I realize I should have told her earlier that our relationship is over but I kept putting it off.

Bradley
February 1: I told Rachel that I met Sheila in town. She said, "Oh, really?" Rae knew about Sheila. I mentioned it was awkward bumping into Sheila and how much happier I am to be with her now. She gave me this big smile and kissed me umpteen times.

Rachel
February 15: It wasn't exactly a fight. No, not even an argument. But it's so frustrating when I want B to act one way and he acts another. And it had to happen on Valentine's Day when couples are supposed to be lovey-dovey.

Anyway, Bradley's friend Dave had texted to see if we wanted to join him and Carla at the dinner theater to see *The Sound of Music.* We were hyped. Carla's cool. She gives off good vibes and keeps us laughing. The show was fantastic. Most of the cast was great; some of those actors should be on Broadway. After the show we stopped to get coffee and pies at that cozy place with desserts to die for.

We started talking about the show. Carla went into detail about how she loved Mother Superior singing "Climb Every Mountain" and how it moved her to tears. Dave said he's seen four Marias and this actress was the best and had an amazing voice. I spoke of how much I loved hearing "My Favorite Things" and how the children blended into so many songs.

And Bradley? Silent. Not a word. Oh, he nodded as we talked but said nothing. So I said point-blank, "Well?" "Well what?" he said. I asked him what he thought of the show. Did he love it? Did he hate it? What? He said, "Not bad. I liked it." That's it. I wanted to squeeze him so more words would pop out. After we got home I asked him again and all he said was "I think these things to myself. I'm not the type who has to tell everybody what I think and feel." It's so upsetting. I just want him to show me his feelings so I don't have to inspect his face for hints of where he's coming from. Reminds me of Dad, who keeps everything inside. Funny that when B talks about the universe and how immense it is, he goes on and on.

Bradley

February 15: Rae got angry with me yesterday after we saw *The Sound of Music.* She keeps badgering me to tell her how I feel. I feel whatever I feel. She doesn't need to know all the time. Sometimes I don't even know. When I have a problem I tell her. Besides, I always let her know I love her chicken dish.

I did love the show, especially when the Captain and Maria sang "Something Good." Very romantic. I've heard the scenery in the mountains of Austria is spectacular. I would love to travel there with Rae some day. The whole show was pretty cool but it ruins it when she always wants me to talk about stuff.

Rachel

February 28: I haven't written for a few weeks. Maybe since B and I talk a lot, I don't need to write as often. He's a good sounding board, though he doesn't always listen and probably never will. I've found if I repeat stuff he gets it. I just wish he'd open up more, but I'm learning to read his body language and figure out his feelings.

Here it is almost a year since we met. Can you believe it? We still have some issues and disagreements. Guess we always will. He's not exactly on time, but he usually texts me when he'll be late.

I'm not perfect either. Sometimes I'm on the phone too long with Kathy or Mom and he stares at me, imitating my jaw with his hand opening and closing. A few times he's taken his watch off and dangled it by his ear to let me know it's time to eat dinner. LOL.

Thing is, I can't ever imagine us parting. He feels the same way. That would be tragic. I'd miss our closeness, the quiet talks, the hugging. We know each other so well. I guess we need to keep finding ways to work things out regardless of how angry we get. We're best friends.

Bradley

March 6: On March 8 it will be a year since I met Rae. I asked if she's willing to celebrate our anniversary by taking a day off work and hiking up this mountain I keep telling her about. It's called Slippery Brown, about an hour north. If we leave early we can get up and come down before sunset. She's eager. It's all set. Wow!

Rachel

March 9: You wouldn't believe the day we had! Slippery Brown Mountain will be embedded in my memory forever.

Bradley prepared the food early in the morning, all neatly packaged in plastic containers to fit into our backpacks: chicken sandwiches, containers of fruits and veggies, and his special chocolate-pistachio cake. He even thought to bring ponchos in case it rained. Our drinks slid into our backpacks. And off we drove as the sun began to rise and the fog ebbed.

We probably moved too quickly up the mountain, because we were huffing after half an hour and stopped to have our first snack. Since it was a weekday, we only passed a few people on the trail.

A ways up we saw a side trail with a sign that read "Butterfly Garden" then followed it until we spotted the garden with a bench. While sitting in total privacy and watching the butterflies whirling about the bushes, we hugged and kissed. If it weren't for the distraction of a mountain to climb, we could have stayed for hours in our secret garden.

Climbing up we saw a few deer and even a red fox running behind a boulder. The fox shook me up, but B took it nonchalantly. It was a longer climb than we thought. We didn't reach the top until 2:15. What a spectacular view! Bradley guessed we could see well over a hundred miles.

At the top we had a yummy lunch and Bradley had a special surprise. He read his anniversary poem to me. I'll keep it forever. The lines beautifully summed up our year together, including subtle references to our arguments, with a touch of humor. It really set the scene for lovemaking.

The hike up was amazing. Going down Slippery Brown was another story. The steep grade was much more of a challenge than hiking up. I had to keep braking myself and my calves ached every step. Also, we experienced the reason for Slippery Brown's name firsthand. Twenty minutes into our descent, the rain began, first gentle and then much harder. We used our ponchos but when the torrents came and gusts of wind blew, our jeans became soaked and our boots filled with water.

The worst part was the deluge turning the trail into slushy, gooey, flowing, brown, yucky grime. I stepped sideways and held on to Bradley's jacket to keep from falling.

Near the bottom I did fall, pulling him down with me. We were a muddy sight from head to toe, like two huge gingerbread cookies trying to get their bearings. All we could do was laugh hysterically. We finally reached the car and wiped off as best we could.

Rachel

March 11: Whenever I go to Bradley's apartment it ticks me off that the place is such a mess. I can't help it. No way am I going to pick up stuff and clean the sink. That's not my job. I worry about roaches or who knows what. So the other day I was on the phone with Kathy telling her about my dilemma, to vent and get feedback. Big problem! Bradley overheard me and became irate. I've never heard him get so angry. Of course I hung up right away. He said it was awful that I would talk to anyone about a problem I have with him. If I'm upset about how he keeps his apartment, I should tell him. He went on and on. Actually, I didn't have a decent response. Truth is, I was afraid of telling him he's sloppy, so I called Kathy instead.

This time I was quiet and just listened to his anger. I did apologize and agreed that if anything bothered me about him, I'd only tell him. I don't know if he believed me. He just said OK. He was very cool and quiet as we ate dinner. But afterwards we saw a funny TV show that got us laughing so I think things are better.

Bradley

March 12: I can't stop loving Rae but sometimes she bugs me to no end. Do you believe she was complaining to Kathy about my messy apartment? I don't usually yell, but this time I could've been heard all the way to the basketball courts. After I calmed down she apologized and promised next time she'd talk to me if she has a bone to pick with me. She even said she wouldn't want me talking to my friends about a gripe I've had with her. Maybe she's finally getting it.

I know I don't keep my place shipshape, but I'm careful about keeping her place neat when I'm there. I admit it: she's a great organizer. That's one reason I like her. When we get married it won't be easy. I'll just have to find a way to manage with her quirky neatness thing.

Rachel

March 18: I realize now that I love Bradley for all the little things he does and says. Yesterday we were jogging in the park and stopped to rest on a bench. A boy, maybe five years old, walked over with his mom to pet Plato. Bradley was so patient with this kid, Seth. He answered Seth's questions about Plato's age and breed. Then Bradley spoke so tenderly, asking lots of questions about what Seth likes and doesn't like. Seth felt so comfortable with B that he went into detail about all the superheroes he loves and the teacher he has in school. I know when we have children, Bradley will be a very loving, kind dad.

Rachel

March 25: Guess what? I'm engaged! YES! No firm wedding date but marriage is in the cards. Bradley and I were on the rug in my living room eating sushi. Then, in his usual quiet way he slid this box between my chopsticks and said, "I think that's yours." I opened the case and there was this beautiful ring with a large amethyst in the center and many smaller amethysts in a gold filigree setting. Just the kind I've always wanted. Some of my friends like diamonds but this is so much more to my liking. It reminds me of violets in a garden.

I called my parents and they seemed pleased. They had already told me what a nice guy Bradley is and they hoped he'd make me happy. Of course, I had to listen to Mom's speech: Do you know what you're doing? Are you sure he's the right one? Don't rush it. She also managed to sneak in that I should set up some rules right away so he won't take advantage of me. I kept saying uh-huh while watching a woodpecker through the window pecking at a pine tree.

Rachel

March 26: I'm so psyched over our engagement, but every once in a while I wonder if I'm up to this. Dating is one thing, but the actual, permanent commitment is kind of mind-boggling. What if we have major differences that we don't know of? That seems farfetched. But are we jumping into something we can't handle? Dan and Kathy should've waited until they could smooth things out more. They kind of rushed it after dating such a short time. Even with a few doubts, I know I'm on board with this. I can't imagine life without Bradley.

We haven't picked a wedding date yet so I won't even think about it for a while. Too early to make plans. I do know that I want an outdoor wedding. It would be beautiful near a lake or the ocean. I even have some music in mind and the color of the bridesmaid's dresses should match the color of the flowers that'll be in bloom. Of course Erin and Missy will take part.

Bradley
March 26: I couldn't hold myself back. If I waited, Rachel might have run off with someone else. We're engaged! Rae and me. Me and she. Us. She's so, so lovely and talented. Whenever I look at her, her eyes sparkle. I can't wait to leave work at the end of the day and meet at her place. She knows just what to say, not only to me but to everyone. I love the way she looks at me and listens to me, really getting into it. So why would I wait?

I called my folks to tell them the news. Mom said, "Best of luck! It's your life and you always make the right decisions." She said she really likes Rachel. Dad said, "Wonderful! You got a prize; take care of her." I talked to George too. He kidded me of course, saying, "Now you've done it. No more girlfriends, no more going out with the guys on Saturday night. You'll be lucky to play any basketball!"

★ ★ ★

Note:
Rachel and Bradley's journals end here, probably because they have become each other's confidant and have little need to continue journaling. Now they are into planning for the future. They will have bumps in the road, but their love story will continue. They have the tools for living a conscious life together with open hearts and open minds that will guide them on their path to vibrant and lasting love.

Understanding Rachel and Bradley's Relationship

Many love relationships begin as Rachel and Bradley's began. We meet by chance. We may find each other at work, at school, or jogging in the park. We may be introduced by friends or attend the same party. Our behavior determines the outcome of our relationship. Because of differences in personalities, values, and experiences, every couple needs to make adjustments to maintain lasting love. Despite our hopes and best intentions, many relationships end with separation and divorce. Long-term success requires that we consciously cultivate our love. To predict Rachel and Bradley's future, we need to examine how their relationship developed thus far and focus on the conflicts, or Power Struggles, they are likely to face and how they will deal with these conflicts as well as how they can apply their strengths as Power Snuggles to maintain a vibrant, happy, and strong relationship over a lifetime.

Power Struggles

The manner in which couples deal with conflicts is more important than the issues themselves. Discussed below are disagreements which might occur in Rachel and Bradley's relationship.

Money

More than 70 percent of couples argue over money (see "Money, Money, Money"), and Rachel and Bradley are no different. Their first conflict is over a parking fee and stems from the couple's prior experiences with money. Disagreements usually relate to a couple's differing values rather than the amount of money involved. Because Bradley grew up relatively poor, he has difficulty understanding why Rachel would pay for parking when free parking is within walking distance to the theater. In contrast, Rachel comes from a household where money is more available and convenience is a priority. For her, the parking fee is trivial, and she considers the convenience well worth the cost. To support their own sides of the argument, they even disagree on whether available street parking is one block from the theater or a few blocks. Even though Rachel and Bradley discuss this issue when it first crops up, it is likely that money will continue to be a contested topic for them.

We cannot determine who will take the lead in handling their finances after they marry. Bradley has the computer skills and the desire to control finances while Rachel is more of a long-range planner. Ideally, they will combine their talents to maintain their budget and plan for the future (see "Who Should Control the Purse Strings?").

Time

Rachel is a stickler for being on time. Before Bradley met Rachel, he rarely had to account to anyone when he was late. Now he realizes that out of consideration for Rachel, he should keep her apprised of when he will be late. He also needs to learn to pay attention to Rachel's anxiety when critical time constraints are involved, such as getting to the airport on time. Rachel, on the other hand, must realize that being a few minutes late to a party will not be catastrophic (see "You're Always Late!"). Though time conflicts won't disappear, Rachel and Bradley benefit by understanding the other's point of view.

Listening to Each Other

Listening to one another is another issue that will remain important over the years. A feeling that you are not being heard in a relationship can be very damaging yet it is impossible to listen to every word our partner says. Recognizing and acknowledging significant information from our partner signals to them that we care (see "A Three-Minute Relationship Change"), even if we don't remember every word our partner shares.

Bradley realizes that Rachel feels devalued and invisible when she gives him important information—as when she told him she would be home late—and he is not listening. Over time, she understands that Bradley means well, but sometimes he is absentminded. Because he wants to please Rachel and he cares about her feelings, Bradley will try to remember issues that seem important to her.

Neat vs. Messy

Rachel is upset when she visits Bradley's messy apartment. She worries that he might bring his untidy habits into a shared space. Since Bradley is much neater in Rachel's townhouse, he will likely be neater in their new home. This does not mean he will always keep their house spick and span, but with his willingness to compromise, he is likely to accommodate her desires. At the same time, Rachel needs to tone down her extreme organizational tendencies. (See "Neat vs. Messy.")

Not Expressing Thoughts

Bradley is an introvert and Rachel is an extrovert. There are great variations in the degree to which one may be introverted or extroverted. Over time, each may move somewhat toward the other's direction. However, their basic characteristic remains the same.

If Rachel refrains from nagging Bradley to talk, he is likely to feel more comfortable expressing himself. But when Bradley is pushed to evaluate *The Sound of Music* performance, he shuts down. Perhaps he feels his opinion is unnecessary. Or maybe he becomes stubborn because he does not like Rachel forcing him to move out of his comfort zone. As we later learn, he has several insightful thoughts about the show, which he records in his journal.

Even though Bradley expresses himself when it feels right, at times stating his ideas is too uncomfortable. Rachel needs to accept that this is Bradley, and she cannot push him to react (see "Say Something!"). A close couplehood requires acceptance of some characteristics that aren't ideal (see "Mom, Marriage Isn't What I Expected").

Interference from Friends and Relatives

As we read, Rachel feels a need to consult with Kathy on ways to deal with Bradley's messy apartment. Bradley's blow-up over Rachel sharing their private issues with others is a warning for Rachel to avoid forming relationship triangles (see "The Facebook Fiasco"). Rachel also needs to control the delicate balance of maintaining a healthy relationship with her mother and respecting the private life she and Bradley build together. Rachel and Bradley need to remain united and place limits on any relatives or friends who try to influence their relationship. (See "Meddling Mom" and "You Love Your Mom More Than Me.")

Sex

Rachel and Bradley enjoy sexual intimacy. Young couples are generally eager and have sex often. However, over the years together, couples may find there are differences in desires, which can cause conflicts. Hopefully, Rachel and Bradley will discover that the secret is balancing sexual needs.

If either partner believes their needs are not being met, problems develop. Level-headed discussions are needed to avoid conflicts that will manifest themselves into other areas. (See "Let's Talk about Sex" and "The Impressive Benefits of Sexual Intimacy.")

Power Snuggles

Rachel and Bradley have many strengths they can use to overcome their Power Struggles and reinforce their long-term relationship.

Their Ability and Willingness to Listen and Respond to Each Other's Bids

Even though Rachel and Bradley experience tension concerning Bradley's ability to listen to what she feels is important, Rachel is able to bring up the issue and receive a positive response from Bradley. Critical to a relationship are partners' responses to bids (see "This Will Always Please Your Partner.") They reinforce our connection and our support of one another.

In listening to and responding to our partner's bids, we also learn about the other's perspective. It is apparent from their journals that Rachel and Bradley wonder what the other is thinking and feeling. Getting into each other's mind promotes understanding and closeness. Even a simple bid such as meeting and holding our partner's gaze encourages feelings of love. Rachel describes how Bradley looks into her eyes, focusing on her when they eat on Maple Street and how it unites them.

Ways They Learn and Grow from Each Other's Interests and Talents

One key to a successful relationship is the extent to which partners support each other's growth in developing new skills and interests. Bradley and Rachel will continue to challenge and expand the other due to their diverse individual pursuits.

- Rachel admires Bradley's cooking skills and knows her cooking could use some improvement. With Bradley as her inspiration, she consults a cookbook and cooks up an entire meal for the two of them. Bradley is thrilled, and he loves the idea that Rachel is stepping out of her comfort zone to try something new. (See "What Makes a Happy Marriage?")
- Bradley admires Rachel's knowledge of plants and looks forward to the time when they can plant a garden together. Gardening has never been his avocation, but he is excited about working with her and learning from her expertise.

- Bradley also brings a third important component to his relationship with Rachel. Plato, the dog, is instrumental in Bradley and Rachel's initial connection and becomes an integral part of their life together. After their difficult fight, Plato becomes the catalyst that reunites them. Pets often help couples soothe over differences (see "Let Your Pet Settle Your Quarrels").

Rachel and Bradley are able to foster each other's unique gifts and share the benefits those traits bring to them as individuals and as a couple. It is of considerable value when people appreciate and benefit from the strengths of their partner, rather than viewing their differences as competitive. (See "The Beauty of Two.")

How They Benefit from One Being a Maximizer and the Other a Minimizer

Supporting each other's growth and learning from each other over the years will prove beneficial to Rachel and Bradley, adding energy to their relationship (see "What Makes a Happy Marriage?"). Rachel, the Maximizer, is effusive, outgoing, and interested in connecting with people. A Minimizer, Bradley always finds office parties a challenge, but he is proud that Rachel can easily connect to his coworkers. Having her there gives him the confidence to let go and even tell a joke. There are also instances when Rachel is comforted by Bradley's more relaxed and accepting ways. She finds him reassuring when times are tough, commenting on how he has such a nice way with words. Even though he is a Minimizer, he adds excitement by initiating spur-of-the-moment ideas, like eating out or hiking up a mountain. (See "Say Something!")

How They Gain from One Being Casual and the Other Being Organized

Every family needs a planner like Rachel, who looks ahead to organize social events, schedule appointments, and keep the household in order. Bradley benefits from her organizational skills. Rachel appreciates that Bradley finds ways to remain calm in difficult situations, taking things in stride. He is willing and able to take care of last-minute details to support her, such as planning and preparing for the hike. (See "Company's Coming!")

Emotional Connection

Rachel and Bradley key into each other's prior experiences, and they are able to find each other's "marble" (see "What Could She Be Thinking?"). Even with different backgrounds, they are learning to empathize, looking for each other's perspective on difficult issues, such as money.

They are also aware of each other's body language and display and reinforce their emotional closeness through touch. Rachel writes that Bradley strokes her back when they reconnect in the park. Bradley is on cloud nine when Rachel dozes with her head on his shoulder as he drives. Rachel notes that Bradley's emotions take over when his eyes tear up as they read *Our Town*. (See "You Don't Have to Say 'I Love You' to Say I Love You.")

Connection to Their Families

Bradley and Rachel's close connections to their families and their willingness to form bonds with the other's family are likely to support them in the future. Rachel wants to emulate Bradley's parents' relationship. She is in awe of the openly warm and affectionate way they relate to each other. Bradley discusses computers and astronomy with Rachel's father, and he even puts up with her mother's probing. They each take the time to develop friendships with the other's siblings.

Although Rachel has issues with her own mother, she tolerates her meddling ways. She knows that her mom wants her to be happy. Rachel keys into her dad's strengths, as well as weaknesses, and she notices similarities between her father and Bradley. She protected her two sisters while they were young, and she continues to be connected to them.

Sensual Connections

Rachel and Bradley enjoy a sensual connection, with frequent hugging, touching, and flirtatious nonverbal language. Because they are comfortable with each other, they will rely on these warm connections during difficult times. (See "The Simplest Way to Warm a Relationship" and "You Don't Have to Say 'I Love You' to Say I Love You.")

Conclusion

Will Rachel and Bradley live happily ever after? Many couples live "ever after" but not happily. They are married for decades, and as they grow apart and dissatisfaction sets in, they may think, "This is what marriage is about. We can't change anything. Our ways are set. We just have to hang in there. Our parents did it, so we can do it."

But our relationship does not have to be endured. It can be enjoyed and lived with loving satisfaction. When both partners are proactive and conscious of each other's needs, their partnership will not only exist, it will flourish. It is never too late to make a change for the better.

And Rachel and Bradley? If they continue their open line of communication, with sensitivity to each other's needs, they will certainly be well on their way down the path to vibrant and lasting love.